T0194946

THAT THEY MAY

HEAR

Christine Dudley-Daniels

authorHOUSE®

AuthorHouse™
1663 Liberty Drive
Bloomington, IN 47403
www.authorhouse.com
Phone: 1 (800) 839-8640

Published by AuthorHouse 07/19/2019

ISBN: 978-1-7283-1657-4 (sc)
ISBN: 978-1-7283-1658-1 (e)

Library of Congress Control Number: 2019908287

Print information available on the last page.

CONTENTS

AUTHOR'S PREFACE

Over the years, African American interpreters overcame many challenges while pursuing a career dominated and controlled by a white American system. This book is not about the racial divide within the interpreting field, but I cannot naïvely or presumptuously dismiss racial aspects that confront African American interpreters in this field. History bears witness that no matter what the profession, African Americans and minority groups have always struggled for their rightful place in their chosen profession. Racist attitudes and stereotyped ideas are often rooted and deep-seated with most people only becoming aware after they are challenged or forced to respond to certain situations or issues.

As a retired Social Work Administrator, my earlier professional studies were in sociology and psychology and over the years I've observed through eyes concerned about a system, a structure, an organism and its impact on a people. I've observed through eyes of a passionate learner who has been a part of this interpreting community since 1995, and a part of this NYC chapter since its inception in 1998. I've observed through eyes of a woman who believes in a God who has created all men equal, while knowing I will always struggle for an equal playing field. It is through these eyes that I have written the beginning years of the National Alliance of Black Interpreters-New York City chapter. It is a reflection of my deep admiration for Celeste (CEE) Owens, Howard Hines Jr. and Kathleen Taylor who entered into a profession that was not always thoughtful or kind. In spite of the many challenges they faced, Celeste, Howard and Kathleen made a commitment to share their skills and resources to uplift the Deaf and hard of hearing communities by motivating and encouraging working and aspiring African American Deaf and hearing American Sign Language interpreters.

Although this volume begins in year 1998, it is important to make mention that prior to 1998; a group of interpreters called "Minority Interpreters for the Deaf" (M.I.D) met regularly to meet the needs of interpreters and students of color. However, it was not until the demise of M.I.D. that two interpreters, Celeste Owens and Sharon Williams, facilitated several meetings at St. Elizabeth's Church in Manhattan to survey an interest in establishing another organization for African American interpreters both hearing and Deaf. I had just finished my studies at the NY Society for the Deaf American Sign Language Academy in 1998 when I was invited to attend meetings at St. Elizabeth's Church. I'm not sure what I expected, but I was impressed with Celeste who was passionate about the field of interpreting and the Deaf community. I later learned her parents were Deaf; CEE as she is known in the Deaf community is a CODA (Child of Deaf Adults). From the moment I entered my first meeting at St. Elizabeth's Church, God's plan for me began to unfold right down to the writing of this book. God had blessed me with skills and over the years placed me in positions to ensure that my skills were developed, sharpened and refined. God was orchestrating my life as well as others who came from various disciplines to join this interpreting community and become committed to the profession. Yes, we brought with us various skills, but we also brought open minds and the desire to provide an important service to the Deaf community. The potential for Black interpreters making a difference in the lives of the Black Deaf community was unlimited. It was about providing access for the Deaf, and educating the wider population, especially the Black hearing population, that Black Interpreters and Black Deaf and hard of hearing communities exist. Much of what you will read may not be indicative of the thoughts of other NAOBI-NYC members. This book is written from the lens of the author, my eyes, my voice, my perception, my thoughts, my analysis and my journey. It is written as a chronological record in which I made every effort to authenticate dates, events and conversations through the review of minutes, flyers, chapter reports, financial records, e-mails, agendas and meeting notes. I also welcomed and received input from former chapter Presidents and members.

Preserving our heritage and sharing our legacy through this writing is my way of acknowledging the people who gave their time and skills to establish this chapter. It is only through knowledge of the chapter's history that those coming behind will gain awareness and respect for the chapter's struggle, identity and true meaning.

I must take this opportunity to publicly thank the late Rev. Dr. Wyatt Tee Walker, Sr. who departed this life on January 23, 2018. I thank him for his support, encouragement and reassurance as we labored to build a foundation for our NAOBI-NYC Chapter, and as I labored to complete this book. My original manuscript was completed in 2010 and I thank Dr. Walker for his assistance and insightful summary.

Chris Dudley and Dr. Walker

It was in 2018, after his death, that I again picked up the manuscript, and before publishing, added a final chapter to finish the early history of NAOBI-NYC. My final chapter also summarizes the author's continued journey from 2008-2018. Although the final chapter and the publishing of this book occurred after Dr. Walker's death, it was my Pastor, the Dr. Wyatt Tee Walker Sr. who recommended the title and it is, in his memory, that I present ***"That They May Hear."***

FROM MY PASTOR

This book is a treasure primarily because it puts on the radar screen of our consciousness a segment of the African American community that has been completely ignored in our advancing struggle of human rights. The deaf and hard of hearing persons in our midst have until now received short shrift or no shrift in our attention to their plight. This community has been left behind because of their affliction and whereas racial prejudice and discrimination has been present, the impact on them has been tangential at best.

The people who are deaf or hard of hearing are victims of a double discrimination. Not only are they members of the African American community, but their affliction has made them invisible and impervious to the gains made by the community of which they are a part. They have lagged behind in information, job opportunities, housing and health care because of lack of access to interpreters which was historically a white thing. This circumstance would have prevailed had it not been for a few pioneering souls who were resilient enough to fight their way through the morass of white dominated interpreter bureaucracy to become certified interpreters to serve a fraction of this underserved community that exists.

"That They May Hear" is a candle of light in this darkness. It details a movement that is answering a crying need to address the plight of the Deaf and hard of hearing community that has been shut out of the gains made in human rights in the last forty years. In recent days, Black congregations have launched Ministries to the Deaf in order to make congregational worship available to the Deaf and hard of hearing in our midst. That is as it should be since the Black Church enterprise has been on the front edge of every positive thrust in Black life. What could be more appropriate since the ministry of Jesus was directed to those who were left out and neglected by society. Better late than never!

The promise of the future looks especially hopeful since this new movement has as its base, the Black Church which is not going out of business soon. It was Christine Dudley's expanded voluntarism that contributed to the genesis of this new movement that holds so much promise for the deaf and hard of hearing community in New York City. Dudley was the moving spirit that created the Ministry to the Deaf at the Canaan Baptist Church in New York's Harlem. She quickly became the lead interpreter at that congregation and as she sought to sharpen her skills, she discovered the great need that existed. Then she became critically instrumental in establishing the National Alliance of Black Interpreters-NYC Chapter (NAOBI-NYC). This volume details that effort. It is a tribute to her sense of journalism, to note the names of those persons who helped to make NAOBI-NYC chapter a reality. That's one of the reasons why this book is such a treasure.

Wyatt Tee Walker Sr. Pastor Emeritus
Canaan Baptist Church of Christ

A JOURNEY BEGINS

Sharon Williams   *Celeste (CEE) Owens*

It began on a hot Friday night July 31, 1998; they came in response to invitations sent out by two interpreters, Celeste (Cee) Owens and Sharon Williams. They came because they understood the importance of belonging to an organization which supported their needs. They came to a room at New York City College of Technology, Brooklyn, New York to establish a chapter for both Deaf and hearing African American sign language interpreters. Many of them were past members of the demised organization: "Minority Interpreters for the Deaf" (MID). They came representing students and they came representing hearing and Deaf interpreters; certified, pre-certified and non-certified.

Certification indicates that a person has met or exceeded a nationally recognized standard of competence in interpreting and/or transliterating. Prior to 2007, there were several certification tests. Most individuals applied for certification testing administered by the Registry of Interpreters for the Deaf, Inc. (RID, Inc) a national professional organization for interpreters. RID administered a written generalist exam and if you passed you were pre-certified with five years to take and pass the performance portion of

1

the exam to become certified with a Certificate of Interpretation (CI) and/or Certificate of Transliteration (CT). RID provided the training to prepare you for testing as well as training to maintain on-going certification through required CEU's. Deaf interpreters or relay interpreters are deaf individuals trained in the profession of interpreting. They are hired to work in conjunction with a hearing professional interpreter and after passing a certification test, the term "Certified Deaf Interpreter" (CDI) is used. The other testing organization was the National Association for the Deaf, Inc. (NAD, Inc.) a national organization established by and for deaf people and who also offered certificate testing for interpreters through a performance exam based on a level of performance, NAD V (Excellent); NAD IV (Above Average) and NAD III (Average). Many NYC African American interpreters took the NAD exams first and then set their goals for the RID exam.

Some who answered the invitation were students enrolled in interpreter training programs (ITP) who were hopeful after graduation; they would be prepared to pass the RID certification test. Some were students enrolled in American sign language (ASL) classes who were focused on improving their signing skills. Some were teachers, social workers, nurses, clerical workers, supervisors and administrators wanting a second career, part time career or changed career. Regardless of who they were or what category you wanted to put them in, everyone who came wanted to develop and improve their skills. I too, was ready to improve my skills while having no idea when I walked through that door, I would be embarking on a whole new journey involving more than skill improvement; I would become totally involved in helping to establish and maintain an African American interpreting chapter in New York City.

National Alliance of Black Interpreters
New York City Chapter

Please join us in our 1st. Meeting on

Establishing a

New York City
National Alliance of Black Interpreters
(NAOBI Chapter)

WHERE: New York City Tech College
250 Jay Street Room 208
Brooklyn, New York
When: Friday July 31, 1998
Time: 6:00 P.M. -- 8:00 P.M.
(Deaf Individuals are strongly encourage to join us)

Please Call us if you plan to attennd:

Friday, July 31, 1998 was the beginning of a long journey for establishing a foundation for this local chapter. Co-founders Celeste and Sharon had already experienced the demise of a previous organization and they wanted to ensure it would not happen again. The idea was to establish a chapter under the umbrella of a national organization which could provide authenticity and support. Our co-founders understood the unlimited potential for Black interpreters making a difference in the lives of the Black Deaf community. *One of the reasons the Black Deaf community lagged behind in information, job opportunities, housing and health care,* Celeste would state, *was lack of access to interpreters.* For Celeste, it was more than being a chapter, it was about educating the wider community especially the Black hearing community. It was about a chapter collaborating, providing training and access through workshops and forums while ensuring that the Black Deaf community had a means of receiving information that was vital for their survival and their progress.

Howard Hines Jr., the Director of NYC Technical College's "Programs for Deaf and Hard of Hearing Students" provided office support and meeting space for the development of this chapter. Over the next several months both hearing and Deaf as equal participants met, discussed and exchanged ideas regarding this new chapter. As I attended these meetings, I struggled to comprehend what this profession meant to those in attendance and to those we would be serving. There were different personalities, and probably different agendas. I wondered how prepared the leaders were for what would probably be a massive undertaking.

We agreed elections would take place in December, but first we had to decide officer titles and qualifications. In the meantime, volunteers would serve as a Steering Committee. Co-founder Sharon Williams volunteered to co-chair. Sharon was a Board of Education Interpreter who had been in the field of interpreting for a long time. She was certified by the National Association for the Deaf (NAD) and a past member of Minority Interpreters for the Deaf (MID). Her demeanor was her strength. She was soft spoken, always polite and encouraging. Sharon encouraged students to utilize and practice their skills interpreting at our chapter meetings.

The next person to volunteer was Andrea Cox who volunteered for the role of Secretary. Andrea worked at NYC Technical College in the office of "Programs for Deaf and Hard of Hearing Students".

The third person was Caroline Taylor another longtime freelance interpreter who volunteered to handle our funds. Caroline had also been a member of M.I.D. and was considered a Religious Interpreter. Caroline also volunteered to chair a religious interpreting committee.

The final person was Wendy Thompson, a National Association for the Deaf (NAD) certified interpreter and also past member of MID. Wendy volunteered to be liaison between New York City and NAOBI, Inc., a very significant role while trying to establish a local chapter. At that time, Wendy was planning to establish her own business and her strong persona stipulated that she would be successful in whatever she wanted to do. These were the officers and chairs who would assist Celeste in establishing the foundation for a New York City chapter.

Wendy Thompson

Our first agenda item focused on NAOBI, Inc. the national organization. Celeste was a member of NAOBI, Inc. and although she was able to provide us with some information, she was not clear what was currently happening within the national organization. Wendy our liaison between New York City and NAOBI, Inc. was asked to investigate. We needed to know more about its current structure; who was serving on the national Executive Board, the name of the contact person we would work with, when they would hold their next election of officers, and finally, if they had a 501 (c)(3) and how New York City could acquire the same not-for-profit status.

While we waited for the national information, Celeste and Sharon were waiting for no one. Celeste set up special interest groups who would share their experiences: CODAS (children of Deaf adults); Deaf interpreters; male interpreters; and American Sign Language (ASL) students. At the same time, she established working committees: bylaws, fund-raising, membership, public relations, newsletter; religious, community access and professional development. Within two months under Sharon's leadership, we had completed the first draft of our bylaws and standard rules. By September, we were ready to recommend membership categories; officer categories; annual dues; name and purpose. Of course, our name would be the National Alliance of Black Interpreters-New York City Chapter (NAOBI-NYC) and our bylaws would follow the guidelines and procedures of NAOBI, Inc. our parent organization.

In November, Wendy reported that the national organization had not responded to her inquiries. Celeste sent an e-mail message to the President of NAOBI, Inc. In Celeste's e-mail, she advised of the group's desire to become a NAOBI chapter while raising questions about the election process for national officers.

Anthony Aramburo, President of NAOBI, Inc. responded by asking for a letter of intent and requested that we contact Leandra Williams, Vice President of NAOBI, Inc. He also advised at next year's conference (1999) in South Carolina, participants would vote for President, Secretary, Eastern Regional Representative and Western Regional Representative. Something else in Anthony's e-mail was intriguing; he indicated that NAOBI, Inc. was in the process of re-establishing itself as a viable organization for African American interpreters and interpreter preparation students. He advised that a bylaws committee had been established to review the organization. *What did Anthony mean about re-establishing itself?* For some of us, his response sparked uneasiness. Celeste, on the other hand, maintained a positive attitude about our future relationship with NAOBI, Inc. and she was adamant about our attending the 1999 NAOBI conference

Anthony Aramburo, was a RID [1]IC/CT and [2]NAD IV certified interpreter with a M.A. degree in "Linguistics of American Sign Language" from Gallaudet University and who later earned his PhD. He had his own private interpreting practice, was an instructor of American Sign Language at Xavier University of Louisiana and was one of the founders of NAOBI, Inc. As I got to know Anthony, I gained a lot of respect for this man's resilience and his commitment to the success of the National Alliance of Black Interpreters, Inc.

Celeste was also committed to the success of the National Alliance of Black Interpreters, Inc., and understood the importance of New York City becoming a part of NAOBI, Inc. and having a say in who would serve on the Executive Board. She knew for our local chapter to survive, NAOBI, Inc. would need to be solvent, and she was going to make sure that NYC members become active participants at the national level.

While we continued to focus and discuss how we would become a local chapter of NAOBI, Inc, Alaina Drake-Mitchell, President of NYC Black Deaf Advocates (NYCBDA), interrupted our thoughts to remind us about NYCBDA's annual Kwanzaa celebration. Alaina was also a member of the new NAOBI-NYC interpreter group and she wanted to make sure there was on-going interaction between the members of this new interpreter group and members of the Black Deaf Advocates. NYCBDA was an organization of Deaf activists who advocated for deaf rights. They not only supported our efforts but were participants in the development of our new chapter. Many of us were members of NYCBDA and looked forward to joining them at their annual Kwanzaa celebration and auction held at the Judson

[1] IC/CT Interpretation Certificate/Certificate of Transliteration
[2] NAD IV – National Association for the Deaf – level 4 (certification)

Memorial Church in New York City. This was not only a supportive effort, but for many who were entering this interpreting profession, it provided an opportunity to interact with the Deaf community. It was not enough to learn American Sign Language and Deaf culture in the classroom, you needed to be in the midst of the people to learn and understand their language and their culture. Culture and language were important in understanding this field and you could not separate one from the other.

Finally, Wendy advised she had contacted National Vice President, Leandra Williams and had forwarded a "Letter of Intent" to NAOBI, Inc. She was also in receipt of a recommendation letter from the National Christian Conference of the Deaf supporting the establishment of our NAOBI-NYC chapter. Wendy advised that Chicago, New Orleans and Washington DC were also in the process of establishing local chapters. *Was this what Anthony's response meant when he said they were re-establishing themselves as a viable organization?* It certainly made sense to have local chapters make up the national organization; but I couldn't help but wonder if New York City had something to do with NAOBI, Inc. suddenly re-establishing itself. It really did not matter; what was important was that local chapters would evolve into an African American interpreting organization, and New York City would be a part of that structure.

Wendy wasn't finished, she had another surprise for us. She advised that we in *NYC would host the national conference in year 2000.* How interesting was that! I was told prior to 1999, NAOBI, Inc. hosted annual *"Summits"* which were normally held at Gallaudet University in Washington, DC. I, therefore, listened in shock while I heard others asking: *How did we wind up with this responsibility? Can we be forced to host a national conference? We* were speechless trying to understand what this meant. We needed an explanation. Celeste and Caroline Taylor tried to provide a reasonable explanation.

At the 1998 "Summit" held in Washington, DC, the question arose regarding who would be willing to host the 1999 "Summit?" At that time, Caroline jokingly stated *we can have it in New York. Well, of course, everyone wanted to come to New York City, and so, most* of the members at the Summit agreed the conference would be held in New York City. Caught off guard, New York City members were forced to caucus and compromise to host a conference in year 2000 instead of 1999. *My goodness*, I thought as I looked around the room, *we are struggling to put together a foundation for a local chapter and now we are called to set up a structure for a national conference of an organization we didn't know that much about. Were they for real?* Well, Celeste was confident we could do this even when the majority of her chapter members were focused on developing a New York City chapter, not a conference. It would mean entering year 1999 finding a hotel, finding presenters, finding interpreters and most of all finding money, WOW! Wendy immediately volunteered to chair the 2000 conference, and she volunteered to apply for our 501 (c)(3) not-for-profit status. The discussion ended, and all we could do was think about our own roles in putting together a national conference, and at the same time developing a chapter.

We ended year 1998 with the election of our Executive Committee. The word was out and our membership started to grow. I could feel the strength and power that was coming together for a common cause. Working interpreters, student interpreters, certified and non-certified all coming together to develop a local chapter of a national organization that would help its members survive and succeed in a difficult professional field. *Did we truly understand our potential as a unified group and with that unity, were we aware of our own power and strength?* At that time, I was not looking for an answer. I do believe those who stepped in to lead such a diverse group faced a huge challenge. We were in a white dominated environment trying to pull together personalities, behaviors and agendas into a unified thought pattern that connected African American interpreters with the African American Deaf community. Self-identity and self- awareness would be critical if we wanted to move forward. We could not wait for others to define us but we ourselves needed to express to the world and to this professional field who we were and what we planned to accomplish.

NAOBI INC BOARD
C.Saundra Toney-Cooley, Pamela Harrison, Wanda Newman, Anthony Aramburo, Leandra Williams, Jackie Bruce (Barbara Hunt not shown)

MAKING STRIDES

Celeste entered 1999 with a chapter ready to work. The monthly business meetings were held at NYC Technical College, Brooklyn, NY, and our Executive Committee meetings were held at my church, Canaan Baptist Church of Christ, in the village of Harlem where the Rev. Dr. Wyatt Tee Walker was Senior Pastor.

Celeste noted the importance of connecting with various deaf groups; we *will be interpreting for people of color* she would state. To ensure our involvement in the Black Deaf community, she put forth the idea of establishing an Advisory Board who would help the chapter stay abreast of events in the Black Deaf community. *They must be able to hear what is happening in the community and advise what they expect us to do.* Our Executive Committee presented guidelines indicating who would be represented on the Advisory Board. The list was confirmed and the following candidates were contacted: AZIZA, Director of Def Dance Jam Workshop, an after school inter-generational company of Deaf, hearing and physically or developmentally challenged artists; Tavoria Kellam, first certified Black Interpreter in New York City; Howard Hines Jr., Director of Programs for Deaf and Hard of Hearing Students at NYC Technical College; Thomas Samuels, Deaf historian and longtime advocate for deaf rights and Pearl Johnson, Executive Director of New York Society for the Deaf. They agreed to serve and meet twice a year with our Executive Committee. We had high hopes that this group of community activists would keep us informed so we could better serve and benefit our Black Deaf and hard of hearing communities.

In addition to having high hopes for our Advisory Board, our NYC chapter committees were taking off with a bang: The American Sign Language (ASL) Committee established to help beginner students develop their sign language skills was growing fast. This committee was chaired by Linda Wilson, an interpreter training program student with Dana Johnson, Chair of our Professional Development Committee providing oversight. Celeste, Howard Hines, Sharon Williams and Kathleen Taylor periodically attended the ASL committee meetings to provide necessary feedback and support. There were complaints, however, that non-members were attending the monthly ASL committee meetings. We had to make sure this group of students understood before attending any of our committee meetings, you had to become a member. While we wanted to be supportive and nurturing to everyone, we needed to follow organizational rules and the most important rule, was membership. It didn't matter to the students, they came and joined our chapter, resulting in a significant increase of a diverse group of student members. To improve their skills, our leaders encouraged the students to attend NYC Black Deaf Advocates' chapter meetings and volunteer to interpret. Members of NYC Black Deaf Advocates were always encouraging and supportive of students attending their chapter meetings to improve their ASL skills while gaining a better understanding of Deaf culture.

Next was the Professional Development Committee established to help us understand our role as interpreters. To start the committee off, Chairwoman, Dana Johnson facilitated our becoming co-sponsor for a forum entitled: "Attitudes Towards Diversity Within Interpreting Community – Can We Really Build Unity Through Teamwork" The presenter was Lourene Gallimore. This was a forum sponsored by City University Consortium Interpreter Education Program (CCIEP); Deaf Advocates for Latino Empowerment (DALE); NYC Registry of Interpreters for the Deaf (Metro RID); NYC Black Deaf Advocates (NYCBDA) and National Christian Conference Association of the Deaf (NCCAD). We participated in the forum and volunteered to work at the registration table utilizing our signing skills to communicate and network with other Deaf and hearing participants.

We also had a Community/Events committee which focused on providing support and training for interpreters. They ensured access to community events for Deaf individuals, as well as raising community awareness regarding the need to have Black interpreters at community events. Kathleen Taylor and Dana Johnson worked together chairing the committee creating plans to improve our visibility in the community. They also kept chapter members informed of community events and workshops and forums for skill development

Finally, there was the Membership Committee, chaired by Pamela Mitchell. This committee provided a chapter brochure, a membership application, a logo, letterhead stationery and envelopes. Her committee also focused on setting up a data base and membership package for new members. Harold Williams a freelance photographer focused on developing a quarterly newsletter called "TERPIN," and finally, a permanent post office box, telephone service and internet service was secured with Charlene Barnett-Forde volunteering to handle our internet e-mail address. We were ready and motivated to move forward.

We were moving fast and Wendy prepared the necessary documents for submission to NAOBI, Inc. Letters of recommendation were secured from NYC Black Deaf Advocates (NYCBDA) and Stuyvesant Association of the Deaf (SAD), with whom our chapter members always supported. Stuyvesant Association of the Deaf was our connection to Deaf seniors. It was a natural progression when you entered this field through NAOBI-NYC chapter that you would immediately be encouraged to interact with these two Deaf organizations. Both organizations were opened to interpreters, whether seasoned or new, attending their activities. They understood the importance of their community having a Black interpreting organization available.

To meet the requirements of establishing a National Alliance of Black Interpreters local chapter, Wendy submitted the following 10 names to NAOBI Inc.

Celeste Owens	Sharon Williams	Kathleen Taylor
Howard Hines Jr.	Wendy Thompson	Christine Dudley
Sharon Johnson	Dana Johnson	Rosalind Hyatt
Charlene Barnett Forde		

Most discussions at our chapter meetings focused on preparation for a face to face meeting with NAOBI, Inc's Executive Board members at the 1999 South Carolina conference. *What kind of questions would they ask and who would answer? Should we have information about hotels and dates regarding the 2000 conference?* We were ready, whatever we had we would use and what we didn't have, we would deal with at the meeting. Celeste, our President and Wendy, our National Representative would be our spokespersons. Celeste made sure all members paid their national membership dues. I looked forward to meeting the Executive Board members of the National Alliance of Black Interpreters, Inc.

While we wanted to spend time focusing on the 1999 conference in South Carolina, Celeste would not let us forget that we still had work to do in our own community. We voted to adopt Def Dance Jam Workshop (DDJW) as a theatrical project. Here was an opportunity for African American interpreters to work with a theatrical group. AZIZA who was a member of our Advisory Board always requested Black interpreters for her group's performances. Celeste and AZIZA drew up a contract which began a long relationship between DDJW and NAOBI-NYC. As a matter of fact, I remember my first experience with DDJW and theatrical interpreting.

Celebrating The 5th Anniversary of Def Dance Jam Workshop
Aziza and Def Dance Jam Workshop
Present

"From Hand To Hand"
Sharing The Message Through Time

Saturday - May 15, 1999
2 P.M. Matinee and 8 P.M.
Tickets: $12 On-Advance / $15 At-the-Door
Children 10 years and under, $5 for the matinee only.

Sunday - May 16, 1999
3 P.M. With a Reception-Buffet following immediately.
Tickets: $25 (Includes Admission to Reception-Buffet)

Aaron Davis Hall
Convent Avenue & W. 135th Street
New York City
(Free Attended Parking)

For tickets, call:
Aaron Davis Hall Box Office at 212.650.7148
Ticketmaster at 212.307.7171

All Performances Will Be Sign Interpreted

Special Performances For School Groups
Thursday - May 13, 1999
10:30 A.M. and 12:30 P.M.
Tickets: $4 for these Special Performances Only
Call 212.650.6900

I received a call from Celeste asking me to meet her at a theatre in Harlem, and when I arrived Howard Hines and Pearl Johnson were there rehearsing for a weekend musical play. Celeste told me I would interpret a shortened version of the performance for school groups on the following afternoon. For the rest of the evening, I observed them rehearsing and said to myself, I *will rehearse all night and be ready tomorrow, I can do this*. I was given the text and went home and practiced. The next day when I arrived, I did not see Celeste and felt anxiety taking control. AZIZA was very supportive and encouraging through the two short afternoon shows, even complimenting me on the job I did. I didn't believe her and when the show was over, I walked home and had a three-day anxiety attack. When Celeste called me to follow up on my experience, I couldn't even talk. Imagine how surprised I was when AZIZA contacted me for another assignment, and even more surprised when I became a part/time member of her staff as interpreter and sign language instructor for the parents of her Deaf dancers. You see, I didn't understand that I had been thrust into the existing field of interpreting. It was NAOBI who helped me see what I was able to do and helped me evaluate and understand what I needed to do to improve my skills. I was always ready to learn and eagerly attended meetings and events with Celeste and Howard. I'm sure I was a pain, but they were patient and never hesitated to answer my questions or share their experiences. They were "mentors" to many who were entering the field of interpreting.

At last, June, 1999 arrived, the date we had been waiting for. Our New York delegation was ready to travel to Myrtle Beach, South Carolina. Kathleen Taylor had another important reason for going; she was taking her certification test in South Carolina. As we traveled, there was excitement knowing we would soon become a New York City chapter of NAOBI, Inc. This was going to be an important weekend. The delegation consisted of Celeste Owens, Thomas Samuels, Kathleen Taylor, Wendy Thompson, Caroline Taylor, Pamela Furline and myself. We were the New York City delegation who traveled to Myrtle Beach, South Carolina.

This was my first NAOBI, Inc. conference and I didn't know what to expect. When I arrived at the hotel, I was amazed. The lobby was full of African American Interpreters and students interacting. I met both hearing and Deaf educators and researchers. I met those with PhDs, master degrees, various certifications and some just having pride and passion. They all came to the conference to discuss issues impacting the African American interpreting community. They were open and willing to share their experiences both good and bad. Although the conference focused on a number of important techniques in the interpreting profession, it was also about supporting each other. It was like a family reunion with a lot of hugs and kisses. It was in Myrtle Beach, South Carolina that I committed myself to the mission of this chapter and to this organization. I was retired and had the time and the desire to learn, improve and be ready to assist in providing a service to Deaf and hard of hearing communities in New York City. It was in South Carolina that we became an official chapter of the National Alliance of Black Interpreters, Inc. The other chapters were Washington, D.C., Alabama, Chicago and New Orleans.

Chris Dudley and Caroline Taylor

There would be no stopping us now. Upon returning from South Carolina to New York City, Celeste decided it was time to officially introduce NAOBI-NYC Chapter to the community. We were ready and we agreed to plan an event with special guests, entertainment and refreshments. Kathleen Taylor and Dana Johnson worked together to put our plans into action. I was appointed Chair of Public Relations and immediately sent letters to Congressmen, Councilmen, Senators, Black organizations and other influential community leaders. It was extremely important that NAOBI-NYC chapter receive support from influential African American leaders.

The National Alliance of Black Interpreters promotes excellence and empowerment among African American/Blacks in the profession of sign language interpreting.

NAOBI - NYC
National Alliance of Black Interpreters - New York City Chapter

Celeste Owens, President

You are cordially invited to our

"OPEN HOUSE"

DATE: Saturday June 19, 1999   2 p.m. - 6 p.m
Place: St. Elizabeth Center 211 E. 83rd Street (bet 2nd & 3rd) New York, NY

Come meet our members, supporters and advocates. Learn about this New York City Black Interpreters Organization for the profession of sign language interpreting

An informative, sociable and entertaining day has been planned
'Refreshments will be served'

Musical Presentations:
Howard Hines Jr. (Sign Language Interpreter)
Darian Burwell-Dew (Deaf Performer)
Aziza and Def Dance Jam Workshop (Deaf and Hearing Dancers)

Special Invited Guests:
Dr. Wyatt Tee Walker, Sr. Pastor Canaan Baptist Church
Rev. Al Sharpton, President National Action Network
Mickie Grant, Playwright

SUPPORTING ORGANIZATIONS
National Black Deaf Advocates
Stuyvesant Association of the Deaf

National Alliance of Black Interpreters - New York City Chapter
P.O. Box 20825   Brooklyn, New York 11202
718 390-7444 (Voice) -718 624-6860 (TTY) NAOBINYC@JUNO.COM

Immediate confirmation came from Rev. Dr. Wyatt Tee Walker Sr, Senior Pastor of Canaan Baptist Church of Christ and former Chief of Staff to Dr. Martin Luther King Jr; Rev. Al Sharpton, President and Founder of National Action Network a civil rights organization where several of us were providing interpreting services; Micki Grant, Actress, Playwright and Composer; Celedonia (Cal) Jones, Manhattan Historian from the Manhattan Borough President's Office and Joseph Jones, former President of an organization for Black Court Shorthand Reporters.

When I gave my report to the chapter, some members expressed doubt about our invited guests showing up. I knew that previous experience had left many believing that most people outside of the deaf and interpreting communities were not interested in Black interpreters or the Black Deaf community. I understood their skepticism, but I was certain what they perceived was not a lack of interest but a lack of exposure and education. I entered this field with little contact and absolutely no knowledge of an African American Deaf community or African American interpreting community. It was on-going interaction with the interpreting field and Deaf community that opened my eyes to a whole new world. What I continued to struggle with was why this Black professional organization was isolated from other Black professional organizations. Wasn't it the same struggles that forced other Black professional organizations to establish themselves? If one mentions Black Accountants or Black Social Workers, no one is surprised. If you say Black Interpreters, the response is "really?" NAOBI-NYC will have to be aggressive and take responsibility for educating and exposing this Black professional field to the wider community. Our "Open House" would be the beginning of the educational process for influential African American leaders in New York City.

On June 19, 1999 we hosted an "**Open House**" at St. Elizabeth Church, in Manhattan. We were amazed and delighted at the community response. Kathleen Taylor and Dana Johnson planned for approximately 75 people with a 30-minute program. It was standing room only as more than 200 participants came to hear about our new chapter and meet our special guests.

Our special guests, Dr. Wyatt Tee Walker and Micki Grant brought members from Canaan Baptist Church of Christ, Rev. Al Sharpton brought his wife and two daughters, Cal Jones, and his brother Joseph Jones, brought their families. One by one, our guests introduced themselves and pledged their support to our African American Interpreting and Deaf community. I don't think they really understood what their presence meant to this community. In any event, we hoped they would see that an African American Deaf community existed, and although this may have been their first exposure to such a vast audience of Deaf African Americans, we will have to make sure it would not be their last. Cameras were flashing and excitement was everywhere. I was Mistress of Ceremony; Celeste presented our mission and purpose while Wendy provided information about our upcoming NAOBI, Inc. conference. Musical presentations were provided by Howard Hines Jr., Interpreter, Darian Burwell-Dew, Deaf performer and Def Dance Jam Workshop. We were excited and could not wait for the opportunity to discuss this event. This large diverse Deaf audience was not only a learning experience for our guests it was also a learning experience for our members. We were energized and moving forward.

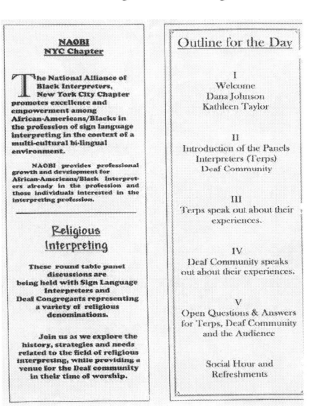

NAOBI
NYC Chapter

The National Alliance of Black Interpreters, New York City Chapter promotes excellence and empowerment among African-Americans/Blacks in the profession of sign language interpreting in the context of a multi-cultural bi-lingual environment.

NAOBI provides professional growth and development for African-Americans/Black Interpreters already in the profession and those individuals interested in the interpreting profession.

Religious Interpreting

These round table panel discussions are being held with Sign Language Interpreters and Deaf Congregants representing a variety of religious denominations.

Join us as we explore the history, strategies and needs related to the field of religious interpreting, while providing a venue for the Deaf community in their time of worship.

Outline for the Day

I
Welcome
Dana Johnson
Kathleen Taylor

II
Introduction of the Panels
Interpreters (Terps)
Deaf Community

III
Terps speak out about their experiences.

IV
Deaf Community speaks out about their experiences.

V
Open Questions & Answers for Terps, Deaf Community and the Audience

Social Hour and Refreshments

The following month Kathleen and Dana collaborated with New York Technical College Programs for Deaf and Hard of Hearing Students to co-sponsor "Religious Interpreting", a round table discussion involving sign language interpreters and Deaf congregants. Both Deaf and hearing from various religious denominations spoke about their own personal church experiences. We explored the history and the needs related to the field of religious interpreting and deaf ministries. As I sat there listening to this insightful discussion, I wished the discussion had taken place in front of my congregation. My Pastor, Dr. Wyatt Tee Walker was supportive of a Deaf Ministry but our Church leaders had little understanding about the professional necessity of the service. At the end of the discussion, a recommendation was made to establish a training tool for Senior Pastors. It was clear that many Pastors and Church leaders were clueless to the needs of Deaf members and deaf ministries. At that time we had relationships with Rev. Johnnie Youngblood Senior Pastor of St. Paul's Community Baptist Church, Brooklyn, Rev. Wyatt Tee Walker, Senior Pastor of Canaan Baptist Church in Harlem and Rev. Nathaniel Lloyd, Senior Pastor of Trinity Baptist Church, Bronx. Before we could think about proceeding with any recommendation, we needed to establish relationships with other churches and Pastors who were providing interpreting services in their churches with little or no interaction with NAOBI-NYC chapter. The big challenge, however, was identifying a Pastor who had the time to spearhead this project of bringing Pastors and Ministers together to be educated about the role of interpreting as a professional ministry in the church. The challenge was, who?

In the meantime, Celeste continued to remind us to attend other deaf and interpreting organizational meetings. *This*, she stated *would ensure organizational support for our chapter as well as keep us abreast of events we needed to support.* Many of us were members of deaf and interpreting organizations and we tried to attend as many meetings as possible. That was not good enough for Celeste, she appointed membership liaisons: Paul Mitchell for Black Deaf Advocates (BDA); Sharon Johnson for Stuyvesant Association for the Deaf (SAD), a senior group; A. J. Jones for Deaf Advocates for Latino Empowerment (DALE); Charlene Barnett-Forde for Registry of Interpreters for Deaf (RID) and myself for Deaf Interpreters Relationship Committee (DIRC). At the same time, Celeste suspended some of our committee activities. A number of committees were dormant and as far as Celeste was concerned *we needed to focus on professional skill development and the upcoming 2000 conference.*

To keep us focused on certification as an ultimate goal, Celeste invited Rob Hills, Coordinator of ASL-English Interpretation Program @ LaGuardia Community College to make a presentation regarding his college's American Sign Language courses, degree programs and Interpreter Training Program. In addition, Celeste presented a workshop on Registry of Interpreters for the Deaf, Code of Ethics - Principles of Interpreting "What I should Know Before Accepting Assignments." Her workshop reviewed, discussed and provided models and situations which applied to the principles of the Code of Ethics.

Suddenly, Wendy decided to step down as our 2000 conference chair. Celeste immediately replaced her with Paul Mitchell, Deaf Interpreter/Deaf Advocate and at the same time appointed Dr. Pamela Furline to establish the process for C.E.U.'s. Dr. Furline would draft "Call for Papers," "Call for Interpreters" and investigate corporate and organizational donations. Celeste knew we needed funds for the 2000 conference, so she appointed Joan Canada to chair our first major fund-raiser. We decided to recognize males in our community who supported our chapter and the deaf community. Our theme was, "Honoring Our Kings." We needed a location, so I contacted my Pastor, Dr. Walker who agreed to let us use the church's catering service and banquet hall to host our first major event. Dr Walker also contacted his friend, TV personality Gil Noble from WABC-TV "Tell It Like It Is" who agreed to be our banquet Master of Ceremony with A.J. Jones as our Mistress of Ceremony.

Four men were chosen as our honorees: (1) **Howard Hines Jr** who had labored in this field for more than 20 years making many contributions to the Deaf community and hearing profession. He had been a mentor, supporter and encourager to many aspiring interpreters (2) **Thomas Samuels,** Deaf Advocate who for more than 35 years advocated for the rights and needs of Deaf individuals. He served on the Advisory Council for American with Disabilities Act and later as Advisory Council for New York State Vocational Rehabilitation Agency. (3) **Rev. Al Sharpton**, one of America's foremost leaders for civil rights. Rev. Sharpton was in the forefront of an on-going battle against economic, political and corporate racism. Since the founding of his organization, he played a major role in virtually every significant move for civil liberty, community empowerment and economic equality. He opened his doors supporting interpreting services and became a friend and supporter of the Deaf and hard-of-hearing community. (4) **Dr. Wyatt Tee Walker** for his social and outreach programs in the Central Harlem community and for opening the doors of his church in support of a Deaf Ministry. This world-renowned preacher and community leader, generously provided necessary support and guidance to our chapter and was a friend and supporter of the Deaf, hard-of-hearing and interpreting communities.

On November 20, 1999 more than 300 participants gathered for "Honoring Our Kings" recognition banquet. They came from as far north as Boston and as far south as Washington, D.C. Michael Jervey, Interpreter and Ellie Kennedy, from Canaan Baptist Church coordinated an all-male fashion show. They reached out into the community and located deaf, hearing and blind male participants for our fashion show. Our male models were Gregory Bell Sr., Robert Grier, Nathan Russell and Gregory Watkins. They modeled African attire by Kilimanjaro Fashions and Ellie's Place attire, Harlem, NY. Def Dance Jam Workshop (DDJW) performed a dance tribute and Michelle Banks, Deaf actress recited a poem as a tribute to the honorees. Harold Williams was our photographer and Sharon Williams, coordinated and recruited interpreters: Christopher Robinson from Boston, Darlene Cabrera, Gerald Small and Rhonda Williams as well as two Deaf relay Interpreters: Tanya Ingram and Alaina Drake Mitchell. The event was featured in the New York Beacon Newspaper. We were again energized and ready to move forward.

Rev Aldridge Miller (for Dr. Walker), Howard Hines Jr.
Tom Samuels and Rev Al Sharpton

Ellie Kennedy and Celeste Owens

Male Models: Nathan Russell, Gregory Watkins, Gregory Bell Sr
Robert Grier

Sharon Johnson and Chris Dudley

Michelle Banks

A.J. Jones, Joan Canada, Gil
Nobel, Christopher Robinson

DDJW Dancers

Immediately following our fund-raiser, we received notification from the IRS that we were approved as a 501 (c)(6) organization which was not acceptable for our chapter. We needed a 501 (c)(3) so we could focus on the educational goals of our African American Deaf community and sponsor programs to educate and seek support from the hearing community. I accepted the responsibility to contact the IRS and re-submit our application for 501 (c)(3) not-for-profit status.

We ended 1999, co-sponsoring with Deaf Women United (DWU) and NYCBDA, a "Christmas Celebration Honoring Deaf Families" at St. Elizabeth's Church in Manhattan. There were also changes to the Executive Committee: Caroline Taylor, Treasurer relocated to Maryland and was replaced by Carol Broughton. Andrea Cox, Secretary stepped down and was replaced by Joan Canada. Sharon Williams, Vice President stepped down and was replaced by A.J. Jones.

During these first two years, it was not easy for Celeste. Everyone who joined wanted to be a member of a successful chapter, but they did not have time to participate in the development of a chapter. Maybe they didn't have time for the nuances of following procedures and protocol; maybe they were seeking certification and employment and could not see anything else or maybe they were too busy and comfortable where they were and saw no need to reach back to help those coming behind them. We were thankful for the core group of members who supported Celeste's vision and made the sacrifice for total participation.

Most organizations large and small have a core group of workers who remain consistent in getting the work done. It was no different for our chapter, it was always an identifiable group who readily volunteered in the planning and implementation of all events. As we grew in numbers, we saw an increase in students. Celeste was good at utilizing students and anyone else who had skills and were willing to work. We were active and we were successful, however, there was an unanswered question which would follow us through the upcoming years: How do we balance providing for the needs of professional full-time working interpreters against the needs of beginners and students? We entered year 2000 trying to answer that question.

Michael Jervey, Nancy Grant, Keri Hayes, Celeste Owens, Howard Hines Paul Mitchell

A.J. Jones, Carol Broughton, Celeste OWENS, JOAN Canada, Chris Dudley

A FOUNDATION IN PLACE

Celeste Owens began 2000 with new members on our Executive Committee. The year opened with us receiving approval from the IRS for a 501(c)(3) tax-exempt status as a not-for-profit organization, as well as New York State and local sales tax-exempt certification. We were now in a position to focus on educational goals for our communities. We had demonstrated the ability to successfully complete activities and we had no reason not to move forward. Our membership had grown and we were financially sound. Our not-for-profit status would enable us to focus on the educational goals within our African American Deaf community and sponsor programs to educate and seek support from our African American hearing community.

The year began with Celeste and Rosalind Hyatt facilitating a discussion on "Educational Interpreting" The discussion focused on the interpreter's role in the classroom which included mainstreaming Deaf children into our public-school system. Although the discussion focused on the role of the interpreters, I was left with unanswered questions regarding the results of mainstreaming Deaf children into the public-school system. What I heard was a child in a room full of hearing children. Other than the interpreter, what other interaction did the child have? I hoped one day I would have an opportunity to raise my questions.

During that time, I along with A.J. Jones and Joan Canada were weekly interpreters at National Action Network (NAN). Rev. AL Sharpton opened his doors to interpreters, students and the Deaf community, and NAN became an ideal and welcoming environment for those of us who were trying to improve our skills. It was at a NAN "Special Educational Forum" with the New York City Chancellor and State educators that I raised a question about research and monitoring results for Deaf children who were being mainstreamed into public schools? We were told *there were no separate statistics* for Deaf children; they were a part of the overall special education statistics. Rev. Sharpton asked me to set up a follow up meeting involving all parties. The Chancellor agreed to attend another meeting to discuss this issue. Unfortunately, the interpreters and advocates who needed to attend were not willing to take the risk of speaking publicly about what was happening in a classroom. No one from the educational arena responded, and I did not push because I understood the consequences if someone divulged information which the Board of Education or the City of New York deemed confidential. I remained patient for another time in the future to share my concerns or ask another question. In the meantime, I had an opportunity through NAN to facilitate the appearance of Pearl Johnson, Executive Director of New York Society for the Deaf on "Court TV" to discuss police misconduct relating to Deaf individuals.

Under Celeste's leadership we continued to sponsor workshops and forums. A number of certified members of the Registry of Interpreters for the Deaf supported our chapter and shared their skills as workshop presenters. We brought in some of the best presenters with Rob Hills, Coordinator of ASL-English Interpretation Program @ LaGuardia Community College helping with sponsorship for most of our workshops. We held our workshops from 6:00 pm – 7:30 pm and business meetings from 7:30pm to 9:00pm.

In addition, it is important to note that many people entered the interpreting profession learning sign language in the church. If they came to NAOBI-NYC, they were encouraged to attend accredited sign language schools and interpreter training programs for a clearer understanding of the professional interpreting service they would be providing to a church. To further help them understand, we sponsored a variety of "Religious Interpreting" workshops and forums. In addition, Rob Hills, of ASL-English Interpretation Program @ LaGuardia Community College supported us with monthly workshops, and to name a few:

> Carole Lazorisak, MA Professor of Human Services presented on "Differences and Similarities of Cultural Values of Deaf Persons and Interpreters Within the Black Community."

Maria Vega [3]CDIP presented on "Working Together: Hearing and Deaf Interpreters in Church, Courts, Hospital Weddings and Conferences."
Lynette Taylor, [4]CI/TC presented a "Voicing Seminar" techniques to improve your voicing skills.

Our workshop participation was great and so were our business meetings. The presenters were some of the best in their fields, and this caliber of presentations was provided on a monthly basis. We felt good, our workshops were open to the community, and many of the participants stayed for our business meeting. Our membership continued to grow.

With all that we were doing, we never stopped planning for our 2000 conference. Planning committee meetings were held at my church, Canaan Baptist Church of Christ and the Skyline Hotel where the conference would be held. The Skyline hotel was a medium rated hotel located in downtown New York City within walking distance of the theatre district. The hotel had been visited by the planning committee and approved based on hotel rates, adequate sleeping rooms and a staff willing to work with us to provide adequate meeting space.

The weekend finally arrived with approximately 120 hotel registered guests and more joining us from the New York metropolitan area. The conference theme was *The Roles and Responsibilities of African-American Interpreters in the New Millennium*" and our keynote speaker was Shirley Childress Saxton of "Sweet Honey and the Rock" inspirational singing group. We had a host of workshops for the conference: "National Multicultural Interpreters Project – "Building Bridges and Crossing Over," "The Role and Responsibility of an Effective Christian Interpreter," "ASL to English Interpreting – Remaining in Control of the Process," "A Shared Perspective: Multicultural Semantics Within a Context," "Black Deaf History: Passing It On," "Legal Interpreting: A Snapshot," "Take One: Principles of Creative Interpreting," "The Next Level: Interpreter Mentoring," "Performing the Art of Sign Interpreting Music" and "So You Think You Want To Be An Interpreter." We were excited and looking forward to hosting our first NAOBI conference in New York City.

---

[3] CDIP – Certified Deaf Interpreter Provisional
[4] CI/CT – Certificate of Interpretation/Certificate of Transliteration

Howard Hines Jr. and Kathleen Taylor

Thomas Samuels with Black deaf advocates panel

At the Saturday night banquet, special recognition and plaques were presented to Stuyvesant Association of the Deaf and NYC Black Deaf Advocates. Our keynote speaker, Shirley Childress Saxton established the Herbert and Thomasina Childress Scholarship Fund to benefit African American/Black children of Deaf adults. The first award would be distributed in year 2001 to help a CODA (Child of Deaf Adult) attend the NAOBI, Inc. national conference in Las Vegas, Nevada. We were proud of our first New York City hosted NAOBI conference and knew we would be active participants in all future NAOBI conferences. New York City was going to be "in the house."

NYCBDA President Kim Lucas & Celeste

Celeste Owens and Shirley Childress

Several months later, we participated in "Deaf Awareness Week," by collaborating with Northeast Technical Assistance Center (NETAC) and City University of NY Interpreter Education Project to sponsor "Interpreting as a Career from a Cultural Perspective." A forum was presented by Howard Hines Jr. and Barbara Hunt, National Eastern Regional Representative from NAOBI, Inc. Barbara, a Certified Interpreter from Washington, D.C. worked as an interpreter for over 25 years in the D.C. metropolitan area and was one of the founding members of the Washington D.C. chapter of NAOBI. When I attended Gallaudet University's intensive American Sign Language program in Washington,

Barbara Hunt

D.C., Barbara who was teaching at the Kendall School (Laurent Clerc Center) at Gallaudet University, invited me to stay at her home. Barbara not only opened her home, but shared wisdom and information you can't learn in a classroom. As a NAOBI member, I met some wonderful supporters, counselors, advisors, mentors and friends; some Black, some white, some hearing and some Deaf. It did not matter where you lived or came from, if you needed support someone was there for you, and Barbara was certainly there for me.

After Howard and Barbara's forum, we continued with "Deaf Awareness Week" supporting NAOBI-NYC Interpreters who interpreted the MAAFA at St. Paul's Community Baptist Church, Brooklyn. The MAAFA, a dramatic depiction of the horrors of the trans-Atlantic slave trade paid tribute to the millions of men, women and children lost in the sale of humans. After supporting MAAFA, we ended our "Deaf Awareness Week" by participating in "Deafest Street Festival" in downtown Manhattan, admiring the booths manned by Deaf participants and enjoying entertainment by Deaf artists.

We were always looking for workshops and conferences that would improve our skills. Joan Canada shared information about an annual religious interpreting conference held in Birmingham, Alabama. In October, several of us traveled to Birmingham, Alabama and participated in "Impartation 2000" sponsored by the "International Institute of Deaf Services" (IIDS). The theme alone drew me to Alabama: *"Because They've Lost Their Hearing, Must They Lose Their Souls."* The International Institute of Deaf Services (IIDS) founder and CEO was Paul William Ellis, Minister/Interpreter and founding member of the NAOBI Alabama chapter. The annual non-denominational conference focused on our specific needs as interpreters in the church. Four days of workshops and worship services were geared to prepare us to adequately interpret scriptures, interpret music and understand the importance of maintaining a holistic Deaf Ministry. The participants and workshop presenters were both Deaf and hearing coming from all over the country.

Paul Ellis

This was my first year traveling to Alabama and my church sponsored me. By the end of the conference, I knew I would become an annual participant whether I was sponsored or not.

After Alabama, Celeste asked me to contact the "Kwanzaa Fest 2000" organization at Jacob Javits Center to let them know we wanted to participate in their Kwanzaa Fest program. They were happy to hear from us and agreed we should become a part of their planning committee for future events. In the meantime, they looked forward to providing access to our Black Deaf community for "Kwanzaa Fest 2000." This not only provided access for our Black Deaf community, it helped aspiring interpreters who needed a forum to apply their skills. We purchased a block of discounted tickets for the weekend and donated them to the Deaf, hard of hearing and interpreting communities. We volunteered to interpret the entertainment segments of the event. We were all over the place providing assistance to Deaf families as they shopped at the various booths. We had such a good time, the following week; we purchased tickets to distribute to our Deaf brothers and sisters for the "Black Nutcracker" a ballet performance musical at Aaron Davis Hall. This performance was sponsored by the Uptown Dance Academy in Harlem. We volunteered to interpret, but it was not necessary, the performance had music without lyrics.

In 2000, we were feeling good. We congratulated Kathleen Taylor who was awarded Registry of Interpreters for the Deaf (RID) certification. We also congratulated Pamela Mitchell who graduated from the LaGuardia Interpreter Training Program. This was a good year and we were winding down celebrating our accomplishments when Celeste breaks our momentum by informing us that she was ready

Celeste Owens

to step down as President. I knew she was tired, but I did not think she was that tired. We were not prepared for the sudden announcement. Having no choice, elections were held for all officers except the office of President. I was elected Vice President and worried what would happen if we did not find a President; I had no desire to be in the forefront of this chapter. We finished out the year with our Christmas Party at the home of Carol Broughton. Howard performed a musical tribute to Celeste and we presented her with an engraved appreciation plaque.

These past three years was a huge task for Celeste. It was her vision, her commitment and her stick-to-itiveness that enabled us to continue in spite of ourselves and our own shortcomings. We came with individual personalities, characteristics and skills. It did not matter why or what baggage we brought with us, we wanted to be a part of an African American interpreting chapter named NAOBI-NYC and Celeste was our first President and it was under her leadership that we laid the foundation for those who would come behind. It was about providing a much-needed service to our African American Deaf community – "That They May Hear."

NAOBI-NYC Chapter

STILL GOING STRONG

Unable to convince Celeste to continue and unable to find anyone certified who wanted to pick up the gavel, Howard Hines Jr. finally agreed to accept the nomination. January 26, 2001, I chaired the first business meeting and immediately held a special election for the office of  President. Howard was elected and became our second President. We had a new Executive Committee with Howard ready to lead and a chapter ready to follow.

At our February chapter meeting we not only celebrated "Black History Month," we decided to have a special "Homecoming Celebration." Invitations went out inviting old and new members to our February chapter meeting: "Come meet and greet our new President, Howard Hines Jr." We had a nice turnout for our homecoming, however, most of the participants were students and beginners. That did not matter to Howard, he enjoyed meeting and greeting. He loved people and people loved Howard. Howard was determined to carry out the goals of this New York City chapter with whomever was available and ready to serve. As I observed him that evening, I could almost see his brain racing, thinking what he will do during his tenure as President

At our February meeting, the founder and producer of IGH Multimedia shared information about her upcoming film "Compensation" featuring Michelle Banks, Deaf actress. Howard encouraged us to see the film and to outreach into the Deaf and hearing communities to let them know about the screening. This was a sensitive issue for Howard. He facilitated a discussion emphasizing the importance of supporting Black Deaf actors and the plight of Black interpreters who tried to enter the Broadway theatrical world. We heard about their frustrations and disappointments trying to find theatrical job opportunities where they could utilize their interpreting skills. The discussion forced us to think and do the math. How many Blacks had we seen interpreting on Broadway and how many Black Deaf actors had we seen in plays? By the end of the meeting we knew we would be there for Michelle. There were two screenings and we supported both.

Michelle Banks

To entice full time working interpreters to our chapter meeting, Howard changed the business meeting time. He believed the membership would benefit hearing from interpreters who worked in the field. For the first 15 minutes, we had an *"Interpreter Profile Moment"* where Interpreters would come and discuss their work experience. The profile moment was successful for a couple of months. It was unbelievable that it became difficult finding Interpreters who would come to encourage aspiring young interpreters. Maybe there were no more experiences to share; after all there were not a lot of African American working interpreters in New York City. Maybe everything that needed to be said had been said. I don't know, I only know at the time we thought it was a good idea. Clearly it was not going to be easy being President and this was only the beginning of frustrating moments for Howard.

Howard kept going and appointed Celeste Owens, Chair of the Skills Development Committee. Celeste immediately started off with a full day forum "Theatrical Interpreting in the Black Community," held in the Amphitheatre on Jay Street, Brooklyn. The four hour panel discussion consisted of AZIZA, Director of Def Dance Jam Workshop, Michelle Banks, Founder/Director of first Black Deaf Theatre Company "Onyx Theatre Company," and Claudia Gordon, first Black Deaf female lawyer in the United States. We were impressed with the large audience of both hearing and Deaf participants. Kathleen Taylor facilitated the discussion by opening up with tips of the trade in a theatrical setting. This was a follow up to our January discussion regarding Black interpreters unable to find job opportunities on Broadway. As the four-hour discussion continued, it became clear that we did not need to go to Broadway for theatrical interpreting when there were opportunities right in our own neighborhoods. There were a variety of community-based theaters with Black theatrical performances where we could make theatre accessible to our Black Deaf community. Perhaps in the future, Black interpreters will have an equal opportunity on Broadway, but in 2001 it was unlikely.

Howard knew what he wanted to do, and by March, 2001 he had established an interpreter schedule for chapter meetings, a quarterly schedule for workshops and forums and a plan for our second fund-raiser. *If we honored our kings in the past* he stated, *it is now time to honor our queens.* He appointed me Chair of our fund-raising committee and we immediately selected six women in our community for their individual efforts, accomplishments and commitment to the mission of NAOBI-NYC: (1) **AZIZA**, founder of Def Dance Jam Workshop, an after school performing arts and academic program for deaf, hearing and physically and/or developmentally challenged adolescents; (2) **Mary Burgess**, leader in the Black Deaf community and founding member of Stuyvesant Association for the Deaf which catered to the needs of Deaf senior citizens; (3) **Pearl Johnson**, Executive Director of the New York Society for the Deaf which serviced the largest population of deaf persons in New York City; (4) **Celeste Owens**, community advocate and professional sign language interpreter who had been responsible for spearheading numerous organizations advocating for the rights of the Black Deaf community; (5)

Kathleen Taylor, advocate for both the deaf and interpreting community who had worked many years as a rehabilitation specialist and counselor for deaf persons and (6) **Iyanla Vanzant**, spiritualist, author, lecturer known for uplifting messages to audiences all over the U.S. and one who always made her lectures accessible to Deaf and hard of hearing individuals.

Before completing our plans for our fund-raiser, we traveled to Las Vegas, Nevada to attend the NAOBI, Inc. national conference. The June, 2001 conference theme was: "Fast Forwarding Into the 21st Century-Preparing Interpreters of the Diaspora." The keynote speaker was Dr. Glen Anderson, first African American Deaf person to receive a PhD in the United States. A native of Chicago he earned his PhD from New

Conference Interpreters

York University in 1982. The conference had a large attendance of a diverse group of Black, white, deaf, hearing, certified, and non-certified interpreters. The conference provided a variety of interesting workshops and forums: "Enhancing Interpreter Competency," "Mental Health Interpreting," "National Testing Preparation," "Preparation for Sign-to-Voice Assignments," "The Art of the Performance," "Discourse Markers of Black Deaf Professionals," "the National Council on Interpreting-What is it? And What Can It Do for Us?" "Mentoring – Do what? Find who?" "Navigating Cultural Diversity in Your Own Backyard," "Interpreting in the 21st Century" and a Student Forum and First Timer's Forum.

We attended as many workshops and forums as time allowed. In every session what continued to emerge was racism and how it was affecting Black Interpreters, especially students. Howard said to me, this *subject must be discussed at our chapter meeting. Our members should know what is happening around the country.* The interpreting field was known to become fierce creating broken spirits and NAOBI-NYC had to be ready to provide support and encouragement for its members. When we returned to New York, Howard immediately opened a discussion at our chapter meeting repeating the stories we heard at the NAOBI conference. The discussion created an atmosphere for some of our students to share their own painful experiences. Although I don't think we were truly shocked, we were surprised to know that students here in New York City were having painful experiences with ITP programs and referral agencies. Whether it was racist or not needed to be explored. It was recommended that we invite heads of interpreter training programs and referral agencies to our meeting for an open dialogue. Unfortunately, this recommendation was not realized and I may be wrong, but I believe in 2001, NAOBI-NYC was not aware of their power to make this meeting a reality.

Moving on, we again responded to members who were interpreting in the Church. Celeste Owens, now Chair of Professional Development made contact with Rev. Emmanuel Sterlin a Deaf Minister who agreed to do a workshop. Rob Hills, Coordinator of ASL-English Interpretation Program @ LaGuardia Community College co-sponsored "Interpreting in Religious Environments" presented by Rev. Emmanuel Sterlin. The Saturday workshop was held at New York Society for the Deaf, in Manhattan. This interactive workshop gave participants an opportunity to practice scripture and musical script analysis. There were so many aspects

Rev Sterling

to religious interpreting that every workshop we sponsored focused on something different. We had a summer break and came right back with a full day forum on "Who Has the Right to Interpret in the Church." This forum addressed the growing number of churches who were providing interpreting services in the NYC metropolitan area. The forum was co-sponsored by NYC Black Deaf Advocates. There were many questions and few answers. There was a recommendation that NAOBI-NYC and NYC Black Deaf Advocates become consultants and workshop presenters to assist churches in providing this valuable service. This meant setting up a plan, a schedule, a structure and someone to be responsible for its implementation and who was ready to do that? No one volunteered.

Still focusing on our religious interpreting skills, some of us again traveled to Birmingham, Alabama to participate in the International Institute of Deaf Services sponsored "Impartation 2001." When we returned from Alabama, we jumped right into planning our November fund raiser. I was Chair, Celeste was Consultant, A.J. Jones and Rhonda Williams were Interpreter Coordinators, Joan Canada was Volunteer Coordinator, Carol Broughton was Treasurer, Kathleen Taylor was Contribution and Outreach Coordinator, Michelle Monroe was Banquet Service Coordinator and Howard coordinated the entertainment. Dr. Walker again gave us permission to use Canaan Baptist Church banquet facilities.

"Honoring our Queens" took place on a Sunday afternoon, November, 2001 in Founders Hall at Canaan Baptist Church of Christ. We honored six women who had given unselfishly of themselves to the Black Deaf and hearing communities: AZIZA, Mary Burgess, Pearl Johnson, Celeste Owens, Kathleen Taylor and Iyanla Vanzant. Howard reached out to Tonya Curtis, motivational speaker who agreed to be our Mistress of Ceremony. The men from Dance the Word Ministry of Canaan Baptist Church escorted our honorees and performed a special dance tribute. Temujin Scott and John Thomas did musical tributes while JASI did a poetic tribute to the honorees. Our interpreters were: John Burgess, Rosalind Hyatt, John Thomas and two Deaf Relay Interpreters, Tanya Ingram and Paul Mitchell. We had a wonderful event with more than 300 people in attendance.

Celeste Owens, AZIZA, Mary Burgess, Kathleen Taylor, Pearl Johnson

Honoring our Queens Committee

Celeste Owens Escorted by Donald Hodo

Mary Burgess Escorted by Edward Green

AZIZA ESCORTED by Rev. David Francis

Kathleen Taylor Escorted by Woody Henderson

Pearl Johnson Escorted by Deacon Anthony Petersen

Howard Hines Jr.

Canaan Men's Dance the Word Ministry

Temujin Scott Musical Tribute

Howard Hines Jr., Chris Dudley, Tonya Curtis

Paul Mitchel, Deaf Interpreter

Tanya Ingram, DEAF INTERPRETER

John Thomas, Rosalind Hyatt, Rhonda Williams

As we closed out the year, we celebrated with NYC Black Deaf Advocates at their sixth annual Kwanzaa Celebration and Auction Benefit at Columbia University. Looking back over 2001, Howard continued to build on a foundation that had been laid while accepting the many changes in the makeup of the chapter with membership being overwhelmingly students and beginners. Although he never gave up, it was a never-ending challenge trying to involve a larger pool of working interpreters. Howard like Celeste was clear about utilizing people who were actively available to the chapter because it didn't matter what category you were in, Howard made it work for the chapter and more importantly, he made it work for our community.

Joan CANADA AND HOWARD Hines Jr.

PREPARING FOR A CAREER

2002 began with Howard narrowing our focus to what was happening in the larger interpreting community. The National Association for the Deaf (NAD) and the Registry of Interpreters for the Deaf (RID) were planning to merge their certification criteria with a number of qualification changes. It was clear we needed to help our members become certified before implementation of the proposed changes. Howard made sure we focused on preparing our members to take and pass the RID written exam. Over the upcoming months, we set up two study groups for the written exam. We even purchased a supply of "So You Want to be an Interpreter" 3rd Edition so members could purchase the books from us at a discount rate. Howard appointed Celeste Owens, Coordinator of the study groups. To join a NAOBI-NYC study group you had to be a member of the chapter, commit to 100% attendance and have a copy of "So You Want to be an Interpreter" 3rd Edition. Celeste contacted Brian Ambrose, BS, [5]CI/ CT, LTA from Professional Interpreter Exchange, Washington, DC, a workshop presenter whose focus was preparing people for the written Registry of Interpreters for the Deaf (RID) test. Rob Hills, Coordinator of ASL-English Interpretation Program @ LaGuardia Community College agreed to provide the grant for our contract and we co-sponsored a full day workshop with an emphasis on the code of ethics. Interestingly, seasoned interpreters we had not seen for some time attended the workshop and several joined our study group and subsequently passed the RID written generalist exam.

---

[5] CI/CT – Certificate of Interpretation/Certificate of Transliteration (American Sign Language Teachers Association)

Many of us juggled our time between the focus group, our interpreting profession and other family and community commitments. There was not much breathing room. This year, Def Dance Jam Workshop performed a photo-musical dance journey "Wonderful Expressions" at the Theatre of the Riverside Church. A.J. Jones, Joan Canada, Gabrielle Johnson, Michael Jervey and I were the interpreters. Kathleen Taylor functioned as our coach. In addition to DDJW, Howard and I attended the graduation ceremony of Miella Bedell and Linda Wilson who completed an interpreter training

Kathleen Taylor with Interpreters

program at the Seymour Joseph Interpreter Training Institute in Staten Island. These two students traveled twice a week after work the long distance to Staten Island for classes while remaining active members of our chapter. Both Miella and Linda volunteered and assisted with every chapter event and meeting. We were happy and proud to attend their graduation and celebrate their achievements.

As we headed towards June, we made plans to attend NAOBI, Inc 2002 conference in New Orleans. Howard was adamant about our involvement at the national level. There were now nine local chapters under NAOBI, Inc: Washington, D.C., Alabama, New York, New Orleans, Chicago, Atlanta, Houston, Detroit and Ohio. There were also active non-chapter clusters representing other cities and/or states. Howard wanted everyone to know New York City was in the house. He even had our members make a list of their concerns so he could present them at the national conference.

Finally, in June we traveled to the NAOBI, Inc. conference in New Orleans. The theme was: "Access for All: Bringing together Culture, Diversity and Leadership in the Profession of American Sign Language Interpreting." The keynote speaker was Carolyn McCaskill-Henry, a Deaf Assistant Professor in the Department of ASL and Deaf Studies at Gallaudet University. There were a host of informative workshops: "Making the Transition from Religious to Professional Interpreting," "Say What You See: A Workshop on Voice Interpreting," "The Multi-Cultural Interpreter101" "Distance Education 101, Interpreting/Transliteration In the 2-Way Interactive Video Setting," "Tax Tips for Interpreters," "Sign Language and the Performing Arts," "Translating English Idiomatic Expressions into ASL," "The Dynamics of Interpreting vs Transliterating," "The African American Black Deaf Community," "The Next Level: Interpreter Mentoring," "Technology and Interpreting," "NAD Forum: The Latest News and Information," and the First Time Forum and Student's Forum.

Jackie Bruce, from Texas was elected National President. Kathleen Taylor was elected Eastern Regional Representative and I was appointed National Parliamentarian. New York City was not only "in the house" but was actively involved at the national level.

Chris Dudley and Jackie Bruce   *Kathleen Taylor*

After the conference and still on our summer break, Howard called a special meeting to let us know he had been asked by NYC Black Deaf Advocates (NYCBDA) to participate on a panel at their summer picnic, Without a question, we would be there to support our President. We attended, socialized, enjoyed the fellowship, food and panel discussion. We left the picnic and attended the Harlem Day events in uptown Manhattan and Deaf Awareness events in lower Manhattan. It was important that NAOBI-NYC members network and socialize whenever there was an opportunity.

During the summer we also heard from Rob Hills, Coordinator of ASL-English Interpretation Program @ LaGuardia Community College. Rob had been supportive of NAOBI-NYC since our beginning and now wanted to donate training material to our chapter. By the fall we had received approximately 21 video tapes of various multi-cultural topics. Howard established a committee to go through the tapes and log them for chapter training sessions.

Our September chapter meeting was quite interesting. To get members more involved in the business aspect of the chapter, I gave a mini-workshop on the "Basic Principles of Parliamentary Procedures." Howard requested that members set up short and long-term goals on how they would achieve certification. *The chapter, he stated, would support their efforts, but they had to do the work.* Celeste announced she had established another organization named *Deaf and Hard of Hearing Parenting Group* and wanted our support. Kathleen announced she had been nominated to the Executive Board of Metro Registry of Interpreters for the Deaf. I announced my appointment as Director of the Deaf Ministry at Canaan Baptist Church in Harlem and finally we announced that once again in October our religious delegation would be traveling to Alabama to participate in "International Institute of Deaf Services" (IIDS) sponsored "Impartation." By now, New York City was well represented at the annual "Impartation" in Alabama for religious workshops and worship services.

When we arrived back in New York City, Kathleen Taylor in collaboration with Malik Melodies Sisterhood, Inc. requested our chapter's assistance in a community based Health Fair. The Health Fair included but was not limited to mammograms, asthma, mental health and diabetes screening. We outreached to the Deaf community to ensure their attendance and we provided interpreting services. It was not often that Deaf people were able to attend interpreted health fairs where information and screenings were free. Prior to the health fair, Kathleen and Joan Canada were the presenters for a mini workshop on medical terminology.

Immediately following the health fair, I informed the chapter of a "No Limits Career Day and Opportunity Expo" for High School Students. This was a reminder that we needed to get out of the "box" into the hearing community to make our name known so people who decide to bring together African American organizations in New York City will have NAOBI-NYC on the list. The Career Fair in partnership with the Borough of Manhattan Community College was hosted by the Urban Network and sponsored by National Black MBA Association; Association of Black Women Attorneys; Black Bar Association of the Bronx; National Association of Black Accountants; National Society of Black Engineers and a host of other Black associations. Although Howard, Celeste and Kathleen agreed to participate, we were too late to register. Networking and outreaching outside of the interpreting field was something we needed to become serious about. We can't wait for people to accidently find out about us; we must define ourselves and aggressively let people know who we are and who we represent. I would continue to push for a more aggressive outreach.

As I look back over year 2002, our membership increased to some 51 members. Full time working interpreters continued to support the chapter financially and some came back and benefited from our workshops and study groups. Howard made sure that we continued to develop our skills and focus on preparing a whole new group of students for the interpreting profession. We saw it as a good year,

MAINTAINING OUR GOALS

Although we would see our membership decrease in 2003, Howard was far from being discouraged. He continued to focus on preparation for certification exams and enthusiastically initiated new projects. Our year began with celebrating Black History Month with refreshments and an "open mike." Howard initiated active working committees: *Workshop Committee, Membership Committee, Fund-Raising Committee and Standard Operating Procedures Committee. We* supported Def Dance Jam Workshop's dance performance, "Spirit Jewels" at Aaron Davis Hall. Joan Canada, A.J. Jones, Gabrielle Johnson and I were the interpreters. Howard and Kathleen provided necessary interpreting coaching. We also celebrated the graduation of Robin LaMour who received her BA degree from CUNY and was also enrolled in an interpreter training program at the Seymour Joseph's Institute of American Sign Language. Howard was adamant about celebrating achievements of our members.

Sometime in March, I received a call from my friend Celedonia (Cal) Jones, Manhattan Historian from the Manhattan Borough President's Office who wanted to attend the NYC Black Deaf Advocates general meeting to inform them about a program he was spearheading. Cal felt it was important that he personally attend their meeting to encourage them to participate in a special event and share their story. At their meeting, Cal spoke about the importance of recording history and asked the chapter to develop a 10-14-minute deaf

Cal Jones

history presentation to be given at the Manhattan Borough President's event. This, he explained, was *about letting hearing people know that Deaf people are ignored and under-reported.* He gave them an outline explaining that the "History Recognition Day" event would take place in June.

While we were thinking about the upcoming event with NYCBDA, Rob Hills, Coordinator of ASL-English Interpretation Program @ LaGuardia Community College, notified us that John G. Lewis would be in New York City doing work for LaGuardia and they were willing to cover expenses for him to do a workshop for NAOBI-NYC. John Lewis, [6]CI/CT had worked in the interpreting field for over 18 years. He had an Associate Degree in Sign Language Interpreting, a Bachelor Degree in French and a Master's Degree in Linguistics from Gallaudet University. He served on the Registry of Interpreters for the Deaf Journal of Interpretation Board of Editors and more importantly was a member of NAOBI Washington, D.C. chapter. NAOBI-NYC co-sponsored "Interpreting in 3-D" with John Lewis providing a clear and concise framework for understanding space in American Sign Language.

John Lewis

After the workshop, we traveled to Philadelphia, PA for the 2003 NAOBI, Inc. national conference. The theme: "Sign Language Interpreters, Interpreter Educators, Deaf Ed. Educator et al: Communicating Effectively through Leadership and Technology Training" The keynote speaker was Claudia L. Gordon, Esq., first Black Deaf female attorney in the United States. This year would be our strongest representation. We attended workshops dealing with technology which was having a profound impact on the interpreting profession: "Video Conferencing and Interpreting," "Understanding Video Relay'/Video Remote Interpreting and its Employment Opportunities," "Teaching in a Deaf Education Program Utilizing Technology," "Interpreting Greek Speak!" "Interpreting in a Technology Savvy Society," "Enrolling in Online Classes," "Let's Have a Good Meeting," the Newcomers, Brotha's and Student's Forums.

On the business side of the conference, Celeste Owens was elected Vice President of NAOBI, Inc. which meant we now had three members of our New York City Chapter actively involved at the national level. Celeste was

---

[6] CI and CT – Certificate of Interpretation and Certificate of Transliteration

Vice President, Kathleen was Eastern Regional Representative and I was Parliamentarian. Prior to our business meeting, I presented the workshop, "Let's Have A Good Meeting" while Kathleen who also served as Chair of the Vendor/Exhibits Committee made sure our chapter secured a booth to display our membership applications, chapter information, brochures and pictures. NAOBI-NYC was in the house.

When we returned from the conference, we attended the event previously brought to NYC Black Deaf Advocates' (NYCBDA) attention by my friend Cal Jones, Manhattan Historian from the Manhattan Borough President's Office. This was Manhattan Borough President, C. Virginia Fields' "First Annual History Recognition Day Awards Ceremony." Cal was happy he was able to include the Deaf community as a part of this project. He came to know about the Black Deaf community through our friendship and he wanted to make sure the wider community knew of their existence. The award NYCBDA would be accepting was called "Underreported Communities History Award." NAOBI-NYC chapter members were excited that the Manhattan Borough President would acknowledge NYC Black Deaf Advocates and we looked forward to attending to show our support.

When we arrived at the ceremony, we found a packed house at the N.Y. Historical Society Building in Manhattan. Politicians, media, philanthropists, educators etc. were all in attendance for this special event. There were eight awards presented and Patrice Joyner, Chair of the Board of Directors of the N.Y.C. Black Deaf Advocates, made a presentation regarding the history of NYCBDA and accepted the "Underreported Communities History Award." The program did not proceed without a hitch. During the event one of the awardees did a narrated slide show presentation and needed to darken the room to enhance the video screen. Suddenly,

Manhattan Boro President C.Virginia Fields & Cal Jones

the lights were turned off creating a lot of noise and a lot of confusion. Finally, someone figured out that turning off the lights prevented the Deaf in the audience from seeing the interpreter who was interpreting the slide show. A spotlight was quickly put on the interpreter and the rest of the program went well. Cal later told me how bad he and his colleagues felt about the incident. He did not want the Deaf community to think he and his colleagues were insensitive. I could only thank Cal for his efforts and hoped he would not become discouraged. This was a Deaf awareness moment, one that we hoped many outside of the interpreting and Deaf communities would remember. We were thankful that Cal remained a supporter providing necessary exposure of the Deaf and interpreting communities to the wider hearing community.

Howard, feeling inspired, began having discussions with producers and writers about Black Theatre projects. There were several plays in production and he wanted to provide an opportunity for theatrical interpreting for our student interpreters. From the beginning, we discussed the potential that we as Black Interpreters had in making a difference in the lives of our communities. Right here in Harlem and Brooklyn playwrights were producing excellent entertaining plays. Through collaboration we hoped to develop an internship program for our members while providing essential activity for our Deaf community. Howard loved the theatre and was an excellent coach. In addition to a theatre project, he contacted Charles Reese, from the American Museum of Natural History, about "KWANZAA Festival 2003" which was held at the museum located on 79th Street in Manhattan. The event was hosted by AKIL, Tammy Hall and Toni Seawright. The museum gave us a block of tickets, which we distributed to the Deaf community. Some of us volunteered to provide interpreting for special entertainment, while others placed themselves throughout the museum to assist Deaf participants. Howard worked with Mr. Reese to make sure we received the necessary materials, proper staging and lighting. We were there in large numbers and we had a large Deaf audience. For our efforts, we received a donation to our NAOBI-NYC educational fund.

We continued to be committed to IIDS' sponsored "Impartation" and our religious delegation again traveled to Birmingham, Alabama to participate in "Impartation 2003" for religious interpreting. When we arrived back in New York we collaborated with Rob Hills, Coordinator of ASL-English Interpretation Program @ LaGuardia Community College, co-sponsoring a full day workshop "Preparing for the Registry of Interpreters for the Deaf [7]CI and CT Certification" The workshop was presented by John G. Lewis, MA, CI/CT and member of the NAOBI Washington, D.C. chapter. The workshop targeted pre-certified interpreters who were interested in preparing for the RID performance exam. We were always searching for tools to help our members and John Lewis was an excellent presenter and resource person.

In December we made plans to travel to Washington, D.C. to support the NAOBI Washington, D.C. chapter's fund-raising banquet "Honoring our Forbearers, Reflecting on Past History & Present Success," which was held at the Marriott Metro Center in Washington, D.C. NAOBI members from Washington, DC chapter always supported our chapter and we were looking forward to going to Washington, DC. Unfortunately, an unexpected snow storm prevented some of us from traveling. We were thankful to those who were able to travel to Washington, DC to support our sister NAOBI-DC chapter.

Through 2003 we continued to be active and vibrant. I was surprised when I received an invitation from the President of the Registry of Interpreters for The Deaf (RID) to accept a two-year appointment on RID's national Bylaws Committee. I was a financial member of RID and their NYC Metro chapter but I was not actively involved. My first inclination was to turn it down, however, between NAOBI-NYC members encouraging me, and learning that Wanda Newman had nominated me, I accepted the appointment. Wanda Newman was an active RID member and also a member of the NAOBI-DC chapter. As explained earlier, RID was the professional organization that set the standards for certified interpreters around the country. They administered the tests as well as provided the training for interpreters to maintain on-going certification through CEU's. During my two-year term, I met and interacted with their Board of Directors along with a number of RID members from various states. What I was exposed to during my tenure helped me understand RID, its structure and its mission as well as put into perspective what we as the National Alliance of Black Interpreters should be doing in this professional interpreting field. I finished my two-year term thankful to

---

[7] CI & CT Certification – Certificate of Interpretation and Certificate of Transliteration

Wanda for facilitating an opportunity for me to share my skills in another arena and at the same time have a wonderful learning experience.

Wanda Newman

Chris Dudley, RID National Bylaws Committee Members

Chris Dudley, RID By Laws Committee at Conference in San Antonio, Texas

The year ended congratulating Kathleen Taylor, coach and feeder for Patrice Joyner (Deaf NYCBDA member) who interpreted the Broadway production "AIDA." We were happy to know that African Americans, whether hearing or deaf, would be interpreting a Broadway production.

Looking back over the year, we did a pretty good job. Under Howard's leadership, we were involved in a number of beneficial projects providing access, facilitating language and developing our skills. We successfully provided essential workshops and forums involving our community. I only hoped that one day we would revisit some of our community projects and follow up on recommendations that were never realized. The year ended with notification from the Internal Revenue Service (IRS) that we would be audited. Our Treasurer, Carol Broughton, Howard and I would enter the New Year planning for our first IRS audit.

New York is in the house

WE'VE COME A LONG WAY

2004 opened with Howard and I making sure all financial and supporting documents were in order and ready to submit to the IRS. We were a new not-for-profit organization and we did not know what to expect from the audit. Our not-for-profit status helped us sponsor workshops and community events and we did not want to lose that capability. After submitting our documentation, we did not breathe until we received IRS notification that everything was in order and we could now proceed with our scheduled plans.

Howard was off and running. He worked out another agreement with Charles Reese and the American Museum of Natural History for "Voices on the Front Line," a performance about HIV/AIDS in South Africa. We had a good experience with this organization last year, and were happy that once again we could provide an opportunity for the Deaf to attend this special Black History celebration. After the event at the American Museum of Natural History, I notified Howard about Evelyn Collins, a Playwright and Producer, at Wadleigh Performing Arts Program and the Harlem Ensemble Company. Evelyn was willing to make her play accessible to the Deaf community. We volunteered to interpret a weekend production of "Born to Sing" which took place in Harlem at Wadleigh High School, Friday and Saturday. Howard not only volunteered to interpret but also coached the team of volunteers: A.J. Jones, Joan Canada, Dianne Smith, Muriel Gaither and myself. This was Evelyn's first experience working with interpreters and she was a little nervous. The actors were high school students and Evelyn wanted to make sure the audience focused on her young actors and not on the interpreters. This was a learning experience for Evelyn and her theatre company, a learning experience for our members, but more importantly, a positive experience for our Deaf community. We were flexible and accommodating. Our goal was not to showcase ourselves but to provide accessibility to a theatrical performance for the Deaf community. Deaf and Hard of Hearing came out for every performance and some saw the play twice. In the end, Evelyn was impressed with the number of Deaf individuals who attended as well as the professionalism of our interpreters.

A.J. Jones, Joan Canada and I continued to interpret Def Dance Jam Workshop's annual performances. The show was entitled: "C D X" Celebrating Differentabilities…..for 10 years. The musical performance included excerpts from the company's annual productions since 1995. Howard and Kathleen were our interpreting coaches. We also congratulated Gerald Small and Pam Mitchell who interpreted the show "Freeda Peoples" at the Billie Holiday Theatre in Brooklyn. Lastly, we were happy to attend an event sponsored by the newly organized Deaf and Hard of Hearing Parents Association established by Celeste Owens. This was their spring fashion show fund-raiser and we wanted to make sure we supported the event. Dianne Smith was the interpreter.

This year our membership decreased again, but it didn't seem to matter; we were doing so many events, Howard discussed purchasing a standard uniform. What better way *to let people know that we were the National Alliance of Black Interpreters-New York City Chapter?*

In April, our national President Jackie Bruce, traveled from Beaumont Texas to New York to present a full day workshop, "Improving Your American Sign Language to Spoken Language Skills." Jackie Bruce was in the profession of interpreting for more than 20 years. She held interpreting certificates and/or licenses from Registry of Interpreters for the Deaf (CI/CT), National Association of the Deaf and the states of Texas and Alabama, a B.A. degree in Deaf Education and a Master of Arts Degree

Jackie Bruce

in Interpreting from Gallaudet University in Washington, D.C. and a completed doctoral work at Lamar University in Beaumont, Texas. She served as a member of the National Multicultural Interpreting project in El Paso, Texas and the Alabama Licensure Committee for Sign Language

Interpreters. Her workshop focused on understanding sign-to-voice as well as videoconferencing and distance education. Jackie loved to teach, and we were delighted that she wanted to come to New York to assist our chapter.

Two months later, in June, our NYC delegation traveled to Hebron, Kentucky for the annual NAOBI, Inc. national conference. The theme: "Interpreting: The Spirit, the Essence, the Goal." The keynote speaker was Fred Michael Beam, Deaf actor, dancer, storyteller, director, choreographer and educator. He was Executive Director of the award-winning organization "Invisible Hands Inc." We also attended exceptional workshops and forums: "Contract and Marketing," "Developing your Smart Business –Entrepreneurship," "Introduction to Interpreting for Multicultural Interpreters," "Overview of the Preparation for the Written Test," "Each One, Reach One: How to Present a Workshop," "Conceptual Accuracy: What they Mean-What You Signed," "Skills & Strategies for Religious Interpreters," "Two Heads, One Interpretation: Effective Team Interpreting," Video Relay: Current Trends, Advantages Issues in the Growing Field of Video Interpreting," and "New Comers Forum," Interpreters' Focus Forum," "Religious Interpreters Forum" and "Students Forum."

NAOBI, Inc. elected our new President Leandra Williams from Chicago, Illinois. Once again NYC was actively involved. Howard was co-chair of "Entertainment" reaching out to members who were interested in "strutting their stuff" in a "Motown Review." I was chair of "Registration" and served as Parliamentarian; A. J. Jones worked on the registration committee and Kathleen Taylor was chair of Vendors/Exhibits Committee. After our NAOBI, Inc. conference, our NYC religious delegation traveled again to Birmingham, Alabama to participate in "International Institute of Deaf Services" sponsored

Leandra Williams

"Impartation" to focus on our religious interpreting skills. We also took the time to congratulate Kathleen who received an "Outstanding Interpreter Giving Back Award" presented by two Connecticut Interpreters.

Time seemed to get away from us. Four years had quickly passed and the presidential term for Howard Hines Jr. was ending. Howard stepped in when we needed a President and carried this chapter for four years. Looking back, we can see that he kept us focused. It didn't matter that our membership numbers decreased, we were developing skills for certification, we were active with our national organization, we were out in the community making a difference and we collaborated making new friends. I'm sure for Howard it seemed like a lifetime. Often, I would see the look of frustration, the same look I saw with Celeste. This was not an easy task; it was a small percentage of the members doing most of the work and we were tired. Some members were working, going to school and had family obligations. I don't know where our strength came from but I know that those who remain were a committed group who was determined to support the chapter. We held our elections and Kathleen Taylor was elected third President of NAOBI-NYC chapter.

Workshop Presenter Fred Michael Beam

NAOBI, Inc Conference
Front: Chris Dudley, A.J. Jones, Howard Hines, Jr.,
Back: Leandra Williams and Uneeda Williams

PROFESSIONALISM IS OUR GOAL

2005 opened with Kathleen Taylor, President; A.J. Jones, Vice President; Uneeda Williams, secretary and I was Treasurer. Kathleen began the year focusing on recruitment. She set a goal to increase membership to 50 members. Immediately, new brochures were made; mass mailing went out, e-mails were sent and hand outs were

distributed. We would focus on the tri-state, New York, New Jersey and Connecticut. Kathleen not only set a goal to increase membership but professionalism and professional skill development were going to be important in everything we did.

For professionalism you only had to observe Kathleen at our chapter meetings and events. She was always on time and her attire, her mannerism and her behavior all made the statement, I *am a Professional*. Kathleen understood if you want people to see you as a professional, you must look and behave the part, and she intended for people to see NAOBI-NYC as a professional organization. Our chapter meetings became professional business meetings. She believed every member had a responsibility to practice professionalism whenever we were out representing the name NAOBI-NYC. Kathleen was unbending on this issue.

For skill development, Kathleen established a "Peer Mentoring Project" (PMP). At each meeting, at least 3 interpreting students rotated practicing interpreting skills as a team. They received immediate feedback and support from Dianne Smith, PMP Coordinator. Yes, in the past members volunteered to interpret at our chapter meetings, however, Kathleen organized this task into an educational goal. The person in the "hot seat" (interpreting) was to have several mentors focusing on different skills of the interpreting process for feedback.

To ensure the best presenters were available for our monthly workshops, Kathleen established a NIA Committee chaired by A.J. Jones, Vice President. These mini-workshops were held after every chapter business meeting. A.J. collaborated with Rob Hills, Coordinator of ASL-English Interpretation Program @ LaGuardia Community College and NYC Metropolitan Registry of Interpreters for the Deaf to seek and invite monthly guest presenters. The NIA Committee was also responsible for planning full day forums and workshops. Kathleen took

Kathleen and A.J.

what we had been doing in the past and enhanced it. To further focus on the importance of the business aspect of the chapter, I, as the Treasurer attended workshops sponsored by the Internal Revenue Service for small and mid-size tax exempt organizations. An Internal Audit Committee was established to annually audit the records of the Treasurer. Laura Taylor was appointed chair of the audit committee.

Kathleen appointed me Chair of the Fund-Raising committee and we decided our next major fund-raiser would honor organizations who supported our chapter and our community. From the beginning we utilized my church banquet hall for all fund-raisers. After much discussion, we decided it was time to change the fund-raising venue. Using a Christian facility had its drawbacks since the interpreting profession was made up of a variety of religious beliefs and denominations. Some interpreters and supporters could not participate because they would not enter a Christian facility. I would spend all of 2005 trying to locate a feasible place to host our next major fundraiser. In the meantime, we continued our tradition of celebrating Black History Month with refreshments and open mike. Our members enjoyed displaying their skills through musical interpreting and looked forward to receiving constructive feedback.

We were more than happy when we learned Jeff Bowden. [8]CI/CT, an active member of the NAOBI Washington, DC chapter was in town. Jeff always made himself available to help anyone aspiring to become an

---

[8] CI/CT – Certificate of Interpretation/Certificate of Transliteration

interpreter. He would just show up and assist where needed. Jeff began his career in deafness as a member of the staff of the Model Secondary School for the Deaf at Gallaudet University in Washington, D.C. He became Program Director at the Shiloh Senior Center for the Hearing Impaired and returned to Gallaudet as one of the first members of Gallaudet Interpreting Services (GIS). Jeff uses an interactive teaching method when facilitating skill development workshops. For our chapter, he facilitated a full day interactive theatrical interpreting workshop entitled "Theatrical Interpreting."

Under Kathleen's leadership, we continued to host monthly mini-workshops collaborating with Rob Hills, Coordinator of ASL-English Interpretation Program @ LaGuardia Community College. We co-sponsored and continued to bring in some of the best presenters in the field. The mini-workshops were held each month following the business meeting: "Powerful Voicing" presented by Stephanie Feyne, [9]CI/CT. and "Voicing" presented by Mary Dunn, CI/CT. Using our training video tapes, we also hosted group workshops on "Receptive Skills" and were always open to holding small group discussions on a variety of interpreting topics. In addition, Christina Trunzo-Mosleh CI/CT, President and Christine Quinton, CI of NYC Metropolitan Registry of Interpreters for the Deaf (Metro RID) were invited for an interactive discussion about Metro RID. Before leaving, they would suggest that NAOBI-NYC and Metro RID collaborate together on future projects.

NAOBI-NYC was now a regular participant at the national level as we traveled to Long Beach, California for our 2005 NAOBI, Inc. national conference. The theme was: "Surfing into the Global Future: Oceans of Possibilities Waves of Technology." As professionals, we needed to keep abreast of changes resulting from technological advances and how to incorporate them into our work environment. Keynote speaker was Sharon Neumann Solow, Interpreter, Interpreter Coordinator, Performer, Lecturer and Consultant. We attended a variety of workshops and forums: "Leadership Training: Unlocking Your Leadership Potential," "Utilizing Communication Technologies to Maximize Your Interpreting Business

---

[9] CI/CT – Certificate of Interpretation/Certificate of Transliteration

Potential," "A Rose By Any Other Name: Culturally Rich Concepts in ASL," "Voicing: Cognitive Analysis," "Not Missing A Beat: A Processed Based Model For Interpreting Religious Music," "Non-Verbal Communication: Image of Body Language," "VI, VRI, VC, VRS: Can You See Me Now," "Plateau to Presenter: Interpreters As In-Service Workshop Presenters," "Work Safely, Maximize Your Earnings, And Feel Great In The New Global Market," "Accelerated Learning Methods to Increase Sign Vocabulary," "What to Know Before You Go…Interpreting in Legal Settings," "Aspects of Video Interpreting: Ergonomic, Interpreting, and Legal Features," "Music" It's Not Just For Hearing Anymore," "I Heard What You Said Now What Do You Mean," "So You Want To Be a Theatrical Interpreter," "Conceptual Accuracy: Moving Beyond Terminology," "A Descripti0on of the Federal-RSA Interpreter Training Program," and First Timers Forum, Brotha's Forum, CDI Forum, CODA's Forum, Educational Interpreter's Forum, Freelancer's Forum, Religious Interpreter's Forum, Student's Forum and Video Relay Interpreter's Forum.

When we arrived home from the national conference, Kathleen established a small committee *to* discuss and review the structure of the national conference. *We want to grow and reap the benefits of conferences,* she stated, *but we also need to think of ways to keep our expenditures at a minimum so we will not have to raise annual dues or registration fees.* Many of our members attended local conferences and forums affiliated with their church and other organizations and she wanted to make sure they could afford to attend our annual NAOBI conference. The committee was asked to submit a list of recommendations on how we can cut conference costs. The committee consisted of Dana Johnson, Laura Taylor and myself.

A.J. Jones was busy making sure we sponsored monthly mini-workshops by collaborating with Rob Hills of CUNY Interpreter Education Project@ LaGuardia Community College. "Dynamic Team Interpreting" Presenter: Dr. Pamela Furline, [10]CI/CT. "Transliterating" Presenter: Jeff Jaech, CI/CT and "Sign Language Interpreting in Higher Education," Presenter Janice Rimler, M.Ed.CT. The workshop presenters donated their honorariums back to our educational fund. Most of them had joined our chapter as supporting members. In the meantime, thanks to Dana Johnson, some of our members were able to take free professional workshops sponsored

[10] CI/CT – Certificate of Interpretation/Certificate of Transliteration

by the Board of Education Office of Sign Language Interpreting (OSLI). These sponsored advanced workshops served as professional development tools to help interpreters in the educational field improve their skills.

My friend Cal Jones, Manhattan Historian from the Manhattan Borough President's Office, attended one of our chapter meetings to remind us that we needed to record the history of Black interpreters in New York City. He recommended that we set up a history club to do research. He was adamant about documenting our history and offered to provide whatever assistance we needed. Everyone agreed, but as I looked around, I knew they would soon forget and our history would be lost. It did not matter, I was clear about the importance of documenting history and I had been preserving all minutes, documentation and notes for future authentication. What was happening in NYC by this chapter was important and I had already began outlining my manuscript.

In November, Kathleen discussed establishing a mixed Advisory Board with Deaf and hearing members meeting twice a year. She asked us to discuss the Board's role as well as implementing a plan by next year's January meeting. In addition, she wanted us to address the fact that full-time working interpreters were not actively involved in the business of the chapter. From day one this has been a concern with every chapter president, and we tried everything. Full-time working interpreters paid their dues and showed up every now and then. They came to our workshops and forums and they were fine with that. We will have to accept that as characteristic of our chapter and move on. Kathleen's final concern focused on Interpreter Training Programs not telling their students about our NAOBI-NYC chapter. She wanted ideas and suggestions how we could reach out to Interpreter Training Programs to get their support. I don't think we had many suggestions; we were doing everything we could to get the word out.

We closed out the year with our traditional Christmas and Kwanzaa celebration and congratulated Kathleen who interpreted the play "Cinderella" at the PaperMill Playhouse in Millburn, N.J. and who also received the "Humanitarian Award" from the Kings County District Attorney during their annual celebration of Women's History Month.

2005 was a good year. Kathleen believed we needed to focus on the professional and business aspects of the chapter. She was focused and determined and in 2005 we had a substantial increase in members.

Kathleen, would now set higher goals to increase our membership to 100 in 2006.

NAOBI-NYC at NAOBI, Inc. Conference
Thomas Samuels, Celeste Owens, Tammy Lane, Uneeda Williams, Ountra Grier,
Pamela Furline, Kathleen Taylor, Chris Dudley, Howard Hines, Harold Williams

CAN WE GO HIGHER

2006, our chapter led by Kathleen Taylor continued to focus on membership, professionalism and professional skill development. Our PMP project was starting to dwindle even though Kathleen and Dianne Smith continued to encourage students to interpret at our meetings. *If you can't interpret in a friendly environment*, they would say, *where do you expect to interpret*? Our meetings were the perfect environment where one could interpret and receive immediate feedback. It did not matter; the project was in trouble.

A.J. Jones, our NIA Committee Chair, continued outreaching to professional presenters. We began with Jeff Bowden [11]CI/CT, our Eastern Regional Representative and member of NAOBI Washington, DC chapter presenting a full day workshop "How to Handle Emotional Situations." Once again, Jeff was available and an excellent teacher and we benefitted from his knowledge and skills. In addition, with Rob Hills, Coordinator of ASL-English Interpretation Program @ LaGuardia Community College, we were able to co-sponsor "Deaf/Blind Interpreting" presented by Susanne Morgan, CI/CT. "International Signing" presented by Bill Moody CI/CT, "Interpreters at the NYC Department of Education," presented by Debbie Swamback, CI/C T and "Video Relay Services" presented by Michael Canale, CI/CT Director of Sorenson, NY. We were providing the best workshops with the best presenters and we were feeling good.

In March, filled with pride, we attended the Humanitarian Award Celebration at the Brooklyn District Attorney's Office in support of Patricia Davis, the Director of the Deaf Ministry at St. Paul's Community Baptist Church, Brooklyn. In addition to recognizing Pat, the Brooklyn

---

[11] CI/CT – Certificate of Interpretation/Certificate of Transliteration

D.A. recognized NAOBI-NYC chapter for providing interpreting services. Kathleen and Robin LaMour interpreted the event.

Not surprising, our President Kathleen was now being sought after to participate in community affairs discussions. The President of LaGuardia Community College sent an invitation to Kathleen requesting that she participate in the President's Round Table community affairs discussions which took place twice a year. We were proud of Kathleen and knew she would represent us well. In addition, Kathleen was invited to several meetings to discuss diversity issues. Racial and diversity issues were always a concern for our chapter members and Kathleen kept the chapter apprised of her various encounters. Imagine someone raising the question, "how do we teach students of color?" What did that mean? Kathleen advised that she facilitated a discussion which she ended by encouraging everyone to seek out workshops which addressed racial concerns. We discussed comments being made about the small number of minority interpreters in attendance at RID conferences. I certainly remembered when I attended a RID national conference, I could count the number of minority interpreters on my hand. Conferences were expensive and many minority interpreters did not work in jobs where they would be sponsored, partially or fully. I know when I attended a RID conference, I was sponsored because I served on a national committee, otherwise I would not have been able to attend. We had already proven that we could sponsor some of the best skill development workshops locally and nationally. If we provided required CEU's to maintain certification, our members would be able to decide which conferences they wanted to attend. It was not about competition, it was about having choices and for most of our members our choice was going to be NAOBI, Inc. national conference where our issues would be addressed.

Kathleen was doing everything to improve our skills as well as provide access for the Deaf community. In collaboration with Malik Fraternal Inc. Alumni Chapter who sponsored a "Home Buying Seminar," we provided access for our deaf community to gain important insight into the housing market. Kathleen and Uneeda Williams interpreted the event and we received a donation for our educational fund from the Neighborhood Housing Services of Woodside NY. We also co-sponsored a self-defense workshop for Deaf women. We provided two scholarship awards and asked the scholarship recipients to come to a chapter meeting to share their experience. The workshop "Self Defense for Deaf Women" was led by Shihan Linda Ramzy Ranson, 6th degree black belt Fuji Ryu Jiu-Jitsu. The workshop was co-sponsored by NY University's Moses Center for Students w/Disabilities, NAOBI-NYC, NYCBDA, Metropolitan Asian Deaf Associates and NYC Metro Registry of Interpreters for the Deaf. One of the recipients came to our chapter meeting to acknowledge appreciation for the scholarship. She gave a moving and emotional testimony and subsequently became a supporting chapter member.

Continuing to encourage ASL students to enroll in Interpreter Training Programs, Kathleen invited Charlene Barnett-Forde and Jeniece Frazier, former students of LaGuardia's ITP program to make a presentation to the chapter about their ITP experience. The presentation went well with relevant questions and leaving several students with an expressed interest in enrolling in an ITP program.

We again traveled to NAOBI, Inc. national conference, this time in Atlanta, Ga. The theme was: "Encouraging Excellence…Evoking Empowerment…Embracing Education." The keynote speaker was Mr. Al Vivian, President, BASIC Diversity and the son of well-known civil rights patriot, Rev. C.T. Vivian. Al Vivian represented his father's legacy well. We were also honored to have Miss Black Deaf America, Deann Reid. We attended a variety of workshops: "Non-Verbal Communication: Image of Body Language," "Deaf Tend Your,' "VRS in Technicolor," "Lift Every Voice and Sing: Working the Script," "The 5th Parameter, The Unsigned," "Discourse Mapping for Educational Interpreters," "A Spotlight on Theatrical Interpreting," "Unlocking the Treasures of ASL: A Study of ASL Classifier Predicates," "The Art of Interpreting Sacred Music," and New Comer's Forum, Brotha's Forum, CODA Forum, Educational Interpreter's Forum, Religious Interpreters' Forum, Video Relay Interpreter Forum and Students' Forum.

At the conference, Howard Hines Jr. presented two sessions on the topic "Lift Every 'Voice and Sing" to prepare a rendition of the "Black National Anthem," for presentation at the closing Sunday breakfast. We worked in small groups, first trying to agree on the meaning of a verse and then going over the various ways of signing the verse. It was awesome. There was a lot of discussion and a lot of tweaking. We finally ended agreeing on one verse for possible interpretation. When we arrived back in New York, Howard recommended that our chapter embark on a project to analyze the text of each verse of the "Black National Anthem." *Perhaps, he stated, we can agree on an interpreted version to be presented at a future conference.* This project was discussed again and again but never got off the ground.

Coming back to New York, we continued to sponsor workshops and forums: "Legal Interpreting" presented by Edwin Ithier, [12]CI/CT; "Religious Interpreting" presented by Howard. Kathleen, presented a full day workshop: "Business of Being an Interpreter." Subsequently, New Jersey Registry of Interpreters for the Deaf, Long Island Registry of Interpreters for the Deaf and NAOBI North Carolina and Detroit Chapters heard about her presentation and requested that she present her "Business of Being an Interpreter" workshop to their respective groups.

The "Peer Mentoring Project" (PMP), continued to have problems. There were only three to four members volunteering to interpret during our chapter meetings. We just couldn't understand why students were not willing to take advantage of the opportunity to put their hands up and receive friendly feedback. Dianne Smith eventually stepped down as Chair. Howard and I filled the gap until a new Chair was appointed.

Kathleen ends her second year with elections and changes on our Executive Committee. Kathleen brought a different perspective to our chapter. We outreached providing services which impacted the Deaf community, we focused on developing our skills, and under Kathleen Taylor we viewed ourselves as a professional organization and continued to climb. She entered her third year feeling good about the progress we had made.

---

[12] CI/CT – Certificate of Interpretation/Certificate of Transliteration

Chris Dudley, Eric Toland, A.J. Jones

Chris Dudley, Leandra Williams

WHERE DO WE GO FROM HERE?

2007 began with changes to our Executive Committee. Robin LaMour was elected Vice President. Tammy Lane, Treasurer, and Kathleen appointed A.J. Jones as coordinator of the Peer Mentoring Project (PMP). We continued to focus on professionalism and professional skill development, and to be clear about our chapter's community outreach projects, Kathleen would state: *We are not a referral service, but a resource who wants the community to be aware that African American Interpreters exist and that we are interested in ensuring access for Deaf people in our community.*

In February, we followed our tradition of celebrating Black History Month by sponsoring a "Family Reunion." We reached out to all interpreters of color to attend the February meeting. We had a good turn out and a wonderful fellowship, but again we did not have a large number of working interpreters. A number of first timers attended our Family Reunion looking for ways to improve their signing skills. NAOBI-NYC chapter would suffice their needs; we were ready and willing to train a new set of students by providing encouragement while hosting necessary workshops and forums.

Robin LaMour, Vice President and chair of the NIA committee began our year with Mary Bacheller Executive Director of Seymour Joseph Institute of American Sign Language presenting "A [13]CODA's Story: A Trilingual Perspective." Mary, the child of Deaf parents gave an inspiring workshop telling her life story of how and why she established the Seymour Joseph Institute. Rob Hills presented on LaGuardia Community College/

---

[13] CODA – Children of Deaf Adults

CUNY's American Sign Language-English Interpretation Program; and Jeff Jaech [14]CI/CT presented "Prepping with parameters: Approaching prep work by considering ASL sign parameters.

For exposure of African/American interpreters Kathleen negotiated an agreement between NYC Harlem's Community Board 10 and NAOBI-NYC to provide interpreting services at their meetings. This would also allow deaf individuals to fully participate in important meetings. Kathleen, A.J. Jones and I interpreted the meetings and Community Board 10 contributed to our educational fund.

The year continued with our members providing access for the Deaf community. Kathleen, Nicole Morgan, Michelle Monroe and Dianne Smith provided interpreting services in Brooklyn honoring the survivors of Hurricane Katrina. St. Paul Community Baptist Church presented "Surprise Witness" the story of Adam and Eve. Howard Hines and Dianne Smith interpreted the performance. Kathleen was interviewed on a Brooklyn Community Access TV (BCAT) show entitled "Miracles." Dianne Smith interpreted and Harold Williams recorded the session. Kathleen also traveled to Bridgeport, Connecticut to join Jeff Bowden as interpreters for "Deaf Awareness Weekend" sponsored by Praise Cathedral Church. Two NAOBI-NYC members, Tracey Lorde and Theresa Dozier, from the tri-state area helped to organize the event. Rev. Job Ayantola was so inspired, he attended the entire weekend. When Kathleen returned to New York, she immediately recommended that we host a Deaf Awareness event for Pastors and Clergy. Unfortunately, we already had a full schedule and could not comply.

In May, 2007 we were so excited because our President, Kathleen Taylor was hired as one of three African Americans to interpret "The Color Purple" play in New York City. The other two African/American Interpreters were Mark Morrison and Jolinda Greenfield. We were beside ourselves with pride knowing that three NAOBI members and the best in the field would be on Broadway. Yes, using African American hands to make "The Color Purple" accessible to the deaf community was what we were waiting for. Everyone was searching for tickets.

Finally, I presented an acceptable 3rd major fundraising program to the chapter entitled: "Recognizing Organizations." We voted on the following

---

[14] CI/CT Certificate of Interpretation/Certificate of Transliteration

honorees: (1) **National Action Network** - (NAN) Rev. Al. Sharpton, President and Founder. NAN is a civil rights activist-oriented organization conceived with a focus on action. The National Action Network is based in New York City with chapters around the country. The Sign Language Interpreters/Advocates Committee of the National Action Network, New York City Chapter was developed to make NAN accessible for Deaf people and to provide a forum where issues of inequality can be discussed involving our Deaf community and interpreters of color. (2) **LaGuardia Community College-ASL English Interpretation**

Rev Al Sharpton

Program – Rob Hills, Coordinator. A student-centered program that is dedicated to developing skilled ASL-English Interpreters. From the very beginning Rob Hills and LaGuardia Community College ASL English Interpretation Program assisted our chapter in co-sponsoring most of our workshops. Many of our members were either graduates of this interpreter

training program or current students. (3) **NYC Dept of Education Office of Sign Language Interpreting-** Beth Prevor Director-OSLIS is an office of the Department of Education District 75, providing Sign Language Interpreters

Rob Hills

for all DOE meetings and events where Deaf people are present. OSLIS maintains an interpreter lab/library where interpreters upgrade their skills. Many of our working interpreters are regular participants of this program's professional lab workshops. (4) **Seymour Joseph Institute of American Sign Language** – Mary Joseph Bacheller, Executive Director. The school is committed to the instruction and Advancement of American Sign Language to both hearing and Deaf communities. Its goal is to produce graduates that have the skill to communicate accurately and effectively with deaf individuals both within and outside of the deaf community. A number of NAOBI-NYC members are graduates of SJI and were only able to continue their studies because of the compassion of Mary Bacheller (5) **St. Paul Community Baptist Church** – Rev. Dr. Johnny Ray Youngblood, Sr. Pastor. In the tradition of the

Mary Bacheller

Rev Youngblood

gospel, Rev. Youngblood designed a socially relevant, thoughtfully crafted ministry that has touched and shaped the lives of men, women and children alike. His Deaf Ministry has a capable team of interpreters, certified and pre-certified as well as signers keeping the ministry totally accessible to the deaf and hard of hearing congregants and deaf community at large. They offer their time and skills seven days a week, making Saint Paul Community Baptist Church totally accessible. (6)

Union County College NJ Interpreter Education Program – Eileen Forestall, is a certified Deaf interpreter who is in her 29th year as Coordinator and Professor of ASL & Deaf Studies. Our New Jersey members recommended this program because Eileen Forestal has been supportive of interpreting students of color.

Eileen Forestal

Our fund-raiser "Wind Beneath Our Wings" was held on September 22, 2007 at the Astoria Manor Banquet Hall, Astoria, N.Y. It was smaller than our previous fund-raisers at my Church's banquet hall, but it was successful with more than 150 Deaf, hearing and hard of hearing participants. I was the Mistress of Ceremony, Howard signed a musical tribute and we enjoyed music and dancing with D.J. Josef Clark. Our Interpreters were: Rhea Ummi Modeste and Edwin Ithier Through the resources of Patrice Harrington and the courtesy of the

Fairmount Hotel and American Airlines, we were able to raffle a 4-day 3-night stay at the Fairmont Hamilton Princess or the Fairmont Southampton, Bermuda for two people in a Deluxe Room.

Leandra Williams

Leandra Williams, National President of NAOBI, Inc. traveled to New York from Chicago for our fund-raiser. Leandra was a special treat for us since we only saw her in her professional role at the annual conference business meetings. It was an enjoyable weekend with our National President socializing on a personal level as we got to know her and she got to know us. Leandra is Registry of Interpreters for the Dea (RID) and National Association of the Deaf (NAD) certified. She had a dual undergraduate major with a focus on law. She received her Master's degree from Gallaudet, University. She is a founding member of NAOBI, Inc and. NAOBI Metro Chicago chapter.

This final year of Kathleen's presidency, brought special congratulations to Robin Renaud and Ountra Grier who passed the NAD-RID National Interpreter Certification (NIC) written exam. This was the new exam that everyone was buzzing about; the result of the merging of certifications from the National Association for the Deaf (NAD) and the Registry of Interpreters for the Deaf (RID). We were proud that our members were fulfilling their goals towards certification. This would also be the last year we would meet at NYC Technical College. Howard accepted a new position as University Director of Deaf and Hard of Hearing Services in the Office of Student Affairs for the CUNY system. We would have to find a new meeting place for our monthly chapter meetings.

We closed out 2007 celebrating the news that Kathleen Taylor had given birth to a baby girl. Unfortunately, the responsibility of a new baby would require that Kathleen step down as President. We were grateful to Kathleen for the professional perspective she brought to our chapter. Our members were heading towards fulfilling their goals of certification and it was important for us to see ourselves as NAOBI-NYC, a professional interpreting chapter.

Robin LaMour as Vice President would have to pick up the gavel. We decided to hold our elections in 2008 and Robin became the next President. The foundation was in place and the next group of leaders would have to stay focused ensuring that the legacy and the goals of this organization continued. Many of us were tired; we had come a long way unswerving as we focused on our African American Interpreters and our African American Deaf community. Even if we felt like giving up, we knew we would need to give our full support to whoever picked up the gavel so we would continue to have a New York

Robin LaMour

City chapter of the National Alliance of Black Interpreters – ***THAT THEY MAY HEAR.***

Front: Kathy Henderson, Diane Boyd, Tammy Lane and Jenette Rosario
Back: Robin LaMour, Dana Johnson, Patrice Harrington,
Felicia Hibbler, and Michelle Monroe

Kathleen Taylor, Robin LaMour, Uneeda Williams, Jenette Rosario, Tammy Lane, Chris Dudley, Diane Boyd, Patrice Harrington, and Howard Hines Jr.

National Representatives

*Eastern Regional Representative
Jeff Bowden and Barbara Hunt
Washington, DC*

*National Vice President
Celeste Owens*

*Eastern Regional Representatives
Kathleen Taylor and
Uneeda Williams*

*National Parliamentarian
Chris Dudley*

A JOURNEY NEVER ENDING

It was at the crossroads of summarizing the activities of 2008, that I put my manuscript down to reflect on the finishing touches for this book. It was this author's intent to complete NAOBI-NYC's early history at the end of Kathleen's presidency which was 2007. The history of NAOBI-NYC was written to focus on Celeste Owens, Howard Hines Jr. and Kathleen Taylor's commitment to developing a structure for this New York City chapter. Although it took a number of years before I again picked up this manuscript, my journey continued, a journey with its own story.

Following Kathleen, in 2008, Robin LaMour became President. After Robin, the chapter operated under the leadership of an Advisory Board. Kathleen would again take up the gavel which was then passed back to Howard Hines for his second go-around. After Howard in 2018, Lisa Lockley was elected President and at the publishing of this book Lisa was still President. Robin LaMour and Lisa Lockley deserve credit for stepping in to grapple with the challenges of maintaining NAOBI-NYC and ensuring that this chapter continued to operate.

Lisa Lockley

When I joined this chapter in 1998, there were many groups meeting and hosting events around the city. We were always involved with other deaf or interpreting groups. At the same time, I could not understand why this Black interpreting organization was not known to the larger society of Black professional organizations. I believe that in New York City, Black Interpreters being a small group were much like the community they served, comfortable in their own created comfort zone and unconcerned about being known outside of their field. I, on the other hand, was always pushing to connect with the wider Black hearing community to let them know of the existence of this Black Deaf and Black interpreting community.

I was attending rallies at National Action *Network* (NAN) when NAN's First Lady, Kathy Jordan Sharpton convinced me to interpret the Saturday rallies. Even with no Deaf or hard of hearing individuals at NAN, it seemed to make sense, and I along with A.J. Jones and Joan Canada became the interpreting team for this civil rights organization. We even extended invitations to interpreting students to come join us at this perfect venue to enhance

Joan Canada, A.J. Jones, Chris Dudley

their skills. Well, not so fast, we were criticized first, for providing free interpreting services and second, for allowing students to interpret without a certified Interpreter present. We knew the standards and the Code of Ethics of the interpreting profession, but it didn't matter, right or wrong we were where we thought we should be. Whether you were Black or white, NAN provided an educational and informative experience that expanded your civic knowledge and challenged your interpreting skills. This was a place where we were comfortable sharing learned language and interpreting techniques. It was a challenge and a blessing and we decided to stay there ready to accept anyone bold enough to join us, and also ready to defy anyone who challenged us.

So, you see, Celeste, Howard and Kathleen faced many challenges keeping chapter members focused on chapter development, chapter accessibility and interpreter professionalism. At the same time, with all of their leadership skills to encourage and motivate, it was basically a small group who followed the visions of our chapter Presidents. In most organizations there is a core group who becomes the foundation of that organization and in NAOBI-NYC, regardless of our strong personalities and faults, we were a part of that core group ready to volunteer to do the planning and implementation of all chapter events. We understood the need to give back to a community and to make the necessary sacrifices to maintain a strong viable chapter. When I think about the forums and discussions, we helped to implement producing a number of sound recommendations and suggestions that we unfortunately were unable to bring to fruition, I could only hope future NAOBI members would revisit some of those recommendations and take them on as chapter projects.

During our early years we enjoyed learning while building and developing a chapter. We traveled near and far taking workshops, going to forums and conferences. We were involved and learning something new all the time. With the increase of technology, video phones, video relay systems, cell phones, texting, Facebook, Skype etc., we would begin witnessing fewer events hosted by Deaf and hearing advocate groups. The increase of technology supported an increase of individualization and another way of communicating and socializing without leaving home. The necessary encouragement and support received at various meetings and events started to become scarce. In an era of expanding technology and on-going changes, future Presidents will have many challenges confronting them. Will they be able to keep members focused and excited about a myriad of possibilities for the Black interpreting profession? I do hope so.

[15]The Bureau of Labor Statistics (BLS) points to increased globalization and greater diversity within the United States as the primary driver of growth for the Interpreter/Translators' profession. They note that demand will likely remain strong for frequently translated languages, with most growth due to greater need for translators in American Sign Language and emerging market languages. According to the BLS, "growing international trade and broadening global ties" will create new jobs for interpreters and translators.

The chapter also experienced many who were entering this field as full-time workers outside of a deaf related field and clearly not ready to leave their steady employment to depend on this interpreting field as their main source of income. Their progress would be slower than those who were decisive in giving full-time attention to becoming an interpreter as their main goal. There were others who had relatively good interpreting skills but they too worked full-time and were juggling limited time schedules. Membership continued to decrease and those attending the monthly chapter meetings were becoming burnt-out, tired or indecisive regarding preparation for certification.

---

[15] USA Today "America's Fastest Growing Jobs" Robert Serenbetz 24/7 wall Street August 30, 2014

As time moved on, Celeste, Howard and Kathleen continued to provide guidance and assistance to help keep the chapter active. Our numerous community activities, however, continued to dwindle and even if there was concern, there were no answers. We continued as though everything was fine. Although my ability to travel had been curtailed by my husband's illness, I continued to be active at the local level, serving on the Executive Board. For years, I along with others had been developing our interpreting skills with some of the best teachers in the interpreting field. I was fortunate and proud to work with and learn from our former Presidents as well as other NAOBI leaders while we labored to build NAOBI-NYC Chapter, but I believed I had now come to the end of that road.

Over the years I came to recognize the many possibilities and opportunities for the Black Deaf and hard of hearing community when supported by Black Interpreters. I wanted to be a qualified interpreter and I understood to become qualified you needed to stay connected to the professional development arena. It may have been my social work background, I don't know, but I believed Black Interpreters had an added responsibility, a responsibility that had to be balanced with the professional arena. What continued to resonate with me were some basic reasons for establishing a Black interpreting chapter. (1) *One reason the Black Deaf community lagged behind in information, job opportunities, housing and health care, was lack of access to interpreters. (2) The wider community especially the Black hearing community needed to be educated about the Black Deaf community. (3) The Black Deaf community needed a means of receiving information vital for their survival and their progress.* Well, it was clear before I continued down that professional road, I needed to re-evaluate my personal goals and decide what path I wanted to take in completing this interpreting journey.

NAOBI-NYC Interpreters had been with the National Action Network since 1999, and it was now time to start recruiting Deaf and hard of hearing people. The Black Deaf and hard of hearing community could use civic and political strength from a strong hearing civil rights organization. An organization who could support and empower them as they went about fighting for their own civil and human rights; a respected organization who could affirm both Black interpreters and the Black Deaf community.

It was not about Deaf showing up or Deaf numbers; it was about Deaf involvement, Deaf pride and Deaf control in a hearing environment. Two Deaf women, Tanya Ingram and Donna Woodie Miles started coming to NAN's Saturday rallies. They were immediately welcomed by community leaders and NAN members. This was a new experience and a challenge for both the hearing members of NAN, the interpreters and the Deaf who came. We were always trying to find the right place to stand and the right seating area for Deaf and hard of hearing people. Tanya and Donna created deaf awareness skits which we performed following NAN's Saturday morning rally. They established sign language classes and people came from the tri-state areas to attend our forums and our sign language classes. As a matter of fact, some students moved on to take accredited courses at LaGuardia Community College and other sign language schools. Those who were serious about pursuing interpreting careers became members of NAOBI-NYC Chapter.

Donna and Tanya

Tanya Ingram and I discussed setting up a Deaf component within NAN and what that would mean for the Deaf community as well as the hearing community. We anticipated criticism, after all, some were still mumbling that we were providing free interpreting services which was not good for the profession, while others felt we were not qualified for the task. It didn't matter, hearing, Deaf and hard of hearing came with enthusiasm about becoming a member of a renown civil rights organization. In 2008 we stepped into unchartered waters believing that the power and strength of a hearing civil rights organization could make a difference for our Deaf and hard of hearing African American community. This was not a job opportunity, an interpreting assignment or an interpreting goal; this was a commitment, a commitment and opportunity to work within a strong civil rights organization to uplift and strengthen a people. A people who had been oppressed, a people who had been controlled and a people if given the opportunity would demonstrate their own intelligence, their own strength and their own ability to plan and control their own life situations. This move would not be good for everyone, but it was a good move for those who accepted the challenge both Deaf and hearing.

The Interpreter/Advocates Committee started with 10 members, only two were Deaf and ready to recruit other Deaf and hard of hearing members. We subsequently established the House of Justice Deaf club and became a team, a committee, a partnership, a club whatever you wanted to call us. Our legitimacy came from being members of the National Action Network, the finest civil rights organization in the country. A civil rights organization where young, old, Black, white, able, disabled hearing, Deaf and hard of hearing people all worked and learned together as human beings exerting control over their own civil and human rights. NAN members who would receive the necessary information to gain a better understanding of their individual voting power and political strength. How awesome seeing Deaf and hard of hearing people coming from various countries and ethnic groups wanting to join the H.O.J. Deaf Club and become active members of National Action Network. I believe NAN was the first hearing civil rights organization to establish a legitimate Deaf component as a part of its formal structure. A component consisting of both deaf and interpreting members.

Interpreter/Advocates Committee 2008
Back (Interpreters): Robin LaMour, Patrice Harrington,
A.J. Jones, Canara Price, Lashun Rogers
Front: Donna Woodie Miles, Deaf; Chris Dudley, Interpreter; Tanya Ingram, Deaf
Not Shown: Lesly Jones, Advocate and Honorable Theresa Freeman, Advocate

By 2011, Tanya Ingram was ready to move the Deaf club to another level. We spoke with State Committee Woman/District Leader and NAN New York City chapter President, the Honorable [16] Theresa Freeman-Timmons about hosting a Deaf Humanitarian Awards banquet recognizing successful Deaf people. Theresa who was also an advocate member of the H.O.J. Deaf Club not only accepted the responsibility to help, but she did everything in her power to make sure their rights would be protected and that elected officials would accept the H.O.J. Deaf Club as an integral part of the Harlem community.

In 2011 the House of Justice (H.O.J.) Deaf club hosted their first Deaf Humanitarian Awards Banquet recognizing five deaf and one hearing person. NAOBI-NYC Interpreters provided the interpreting service. Recipients received a plaque from the Rev Al Sharpton and H.O.J. Deaf club, and certificates from Harlem's political leaders. The House of Justice Deaf Club received special congressional recognition for their commitment to strengthen our community through volunteer services which was presented at the Congress of the United States House of Representatives to the Fifteenth-Congressional District of NYC of the 112th Congress first session. This was the beginning of our annual Deaf Humanitarian Awards Banquet which became the vehicle the Honorable Theresa Freeman delighted in using to ensure that Harlem elected officials expressed their appreciation to Deaf honorees for their service and achievement. After her death, Harlem leaders and politicians continued to support and recognize the H.O.J. Deaf Club and their honorees.

Membership continued to increase and Deaf people came to the Saturday NAN rallies and we interpreted. Deaf and hard of hearing were involved in NAN marches in Washington, DC and New York City where we interpreted, and even got arrested. H.O.J. Deaf Club began holding their business meetings every Tuesday evening as well as weekly sign language classes. Every month, they sponsored free workshops or

---

[16] Honorable Theresa Freeman-Timmons departed this life February 3, 2015. She is remembered annually at our Awards banquet with an award presented to a hearing person for their support to the Deaf community.

forums that impacted the Deaf and hard of hearing community, and we interpreted. Every month we interpreted NAN's "Legal Night" opened to the public where lawyers gave free legal counsel to anyone, hearing or deaf with a problem. The Director of NAN's Crisis department set up special hours to deal with Deaf concerns regarding housing issues, landlord issues, employment concerns, discrimination, etc. Bi-monthly, the Deaf Club sponsored Deaf entertainment in partnership with a music venue located in Harlem entertaining both a hearing and Deaf audience, and we interpreted. Our Deaf members boasted about shaking the hand of U.S. President Barack Obama at NAN's annual national convention, and yes, we interpreted. Finally, in 2018, in celebration of the Deaf Club's tenth anniversary, the Manhattan Borough President Gale E. Brewer, designated Saturday February 10th as *"H.O.J. Deaf Club day"* in the borough of Manhattan.

As of 2018, H.O.J. Deaf Club was some 48 members strong with the majority being Deaf and hard of hearing supported by interpreters and advocates. NAOBI-NYC interpreters were and probably will continue to be a very busy group supporting a very busy group of Deaf and hard of hearing civil rights members. We are thankful to all NAOBI and RID Interpreters who volunteered their time and their skills to offer support. While NAOBI-NYC chapter continues to help develop and inspire interpreters, we who are members of National Action Network will continue to use our power, our strength and our ability to support the uplifting of our Deaf and hard of hearing community. While Deaf and hard of hearing members of the National Action Network continue to be proud of their community work, political networking and noted accomplishments, we, who are their partners will continue to be thankful for the opportunity to work with them. With that being said, a Black interpreter's journey is far from being over *"**That They May Hear.**"*

Deaf Interpreter Tanya Ingram with
Honorable Charlie Rangel

Chris Dudley and
Rev Al Sharpton
President/Founder NAN

Tanya Ingram & Chris Dudley
Rev. Herbert Daughtry

Chris Dudley, A.J. Jones, Lisa Lockley

HOUSE OF JUSTICE DEAF CLUB BANQUET

Kathleen Taylor with Michael Hardy, Esq
Exec Vice President NAN

Howard Hines Jr

Wendy Thompson and Kathleen Taylor

Jasper Thacker Bowell and
Honorable Theresa Freeman

Wendy Thompson, Interpreter with
Deaf members receiving plaques
from Community Leaders: Jeff
Eaton, President Mid-Manhattan
NAACP & Chief of Staff to
Congressman Charles Rangel;
Honorable Theresa Freeman
State Committee Wilma Brown,
District Leader; and Bill Griffin
President NAN NYC Chapter

DEAF PARTICIPANTS AT A H.O.J.
DEAF CLUB EVENT

NAOBI-NYC INTERPRETERS at NAN CONVENTION

Back Row: A.J. Jones, Lisa Lockley, Tavoria Kellum, Sandra Campblell-Jeffries
Middle Row: Tanya Ingram, Patrice Creamer, Guest Presenter Talila Lewis
Bottom Row: Diane Smith, Chris Dudley, Sharon Johnson, Canara Price

DEAF PARTICIPANTS AT NAN CONVENTION

From Back: Nicolyn Plummer; Donna Woodie Miles; Melvin Creamer; Ike
Williams; Opal GORDON; Tanya Ingram; Marsellette Davis; Jennifer
Bailey; Magdalena Almanzar; Adrianne Jennings; Amina Maycock;
Patrice Creamer; Sandra Rivers; Capricia Avery; James Huff

PRESIDENT PROFILES ANNUAL LIST OF ACTIVE MEMBERS

Celeste Owens, President - 1998 - 2000

Co-founder and first President, Celeste Owens, native of New York City was a community advocate who always fought for the rights of deaf persons or coordinated services to meet their specific needs. At the time she served as President, Celeste, a CODA (Child of Deaf Adults) was a certified National Association for the Deaf (NAD V) Sign Language Interpreter. She also holds NIC certification with the Registry of Interpreters for the Deaf (RID).

An entrepreneur, Celeste has served as President and Founder of Deaf Enterprises, interpreter in the classroom, legal situations and the medical professions. She has also worked in the theatrical interpreting community in Broadway productions.

She was also the founder of Stuyvesant Association of the Deaf (SAD) and served as Acting Director for the National Black Deaf Advocates (NBDA), the first hearing person to hold that position in a predominantly national deaf organization. Celeste was responsible for coordinating a parent's support group (MELD) and sponsored many community events for the deaf. She is Founder of NYC Deaf & Hard of Hearing Parents Association (NYCDHHPA), Cultural Educational Entertainment Sign Language Network (CSLN) and CODAs of Color (COC).

CEE's 3-year tenure as President of NAOBI-NYC focused on ensuring a strong foundation for the New York City chapter. She emphasized the inclusion of the Deaf community in the local chapter's structure. After her tenure as President, she was elected and served as Vice President of National Alliance of Black Interpreters, Inc. (NAOBI, Inc.)

CEE as she is known in the Deaf Community is married to Mr. Thomas Samuels, Deaf Historian and she is the mother of two children and one Deaf foster son.

YEAR 1998

Celeste Owens - Chair

Sharon Williams – Co-Chair

Charlene Barnett-Forde
Barbara Benjamin
Joan Canada
Andrea Cox
Roodeline Daniel
Christine Dudley
Marilyn Edwards
Curtis Harris
Howard Hines Jr.
Michael Jervey
Wendy Thompson

Dana Johnson
Sharon Johnson
A.J. Jones
Annie Lee
Alaina Drake Mitchell
Pamela Mitchell
Gerald Small
Dexter Sylvester
Caroline Taylor
Kathleen Taylor

YEAR 1999 - 44 Financial MEMBERS

Officers:

President	Celeste Owens
Vice President	Sharon Williams
Secretary	Andrea Cox
Treasurer	Caroline Taylor
National Rep	Wendy Thompson
Associate Rep	Dana Johnson
Deaf Rep	Alaina Drake Mitchell
Parliamentarian	Christine Dudley
Member-at-Large	Pam Mitchell
Member-at-Large	Paul Mitchell
Member-at-Large	Sharon Johnson
Member-at-Large	Curtis Harris

Community Advisory Board: AZIZA Tavoria Kellam Howard Hines Thomas Samuel Pearl Johnson

Membership

Miella Bedell	A.J. Jones
Barbara Benjamin	Annie Lee
Carol Broughton	Gary Mitchell
Charlene Barnett-Forde	Michelle Monroe
Barbara Ann Braithwaite	Lucia Rodney
Joan Canada	Gerald Small C
Pamela Furline	Dianne Smith
Nancy Grant	Dexter Sylvester
Sugar Harris	Donna Sylvester
Catherine Hayes	Kathleen Taylor

Keri Hayes

Helen Horne

Rosalind Hyatt

Sharon Johnson

Harold Williams

Rhonda Williams

Linda Wilson

YEAR 2000 - 49 Financial Members

Officers:

President:	Celeste Owens
Vice President	A.J. Jones
Secretary	Joan Canada
Treasurer	Carol Broughton
Parliamentarian	Christine Dudley
Member-at-Large	Sharon Johnson
Member-at-Large	Linda Wilson

Advisory Board: Tavoria Kellam Howard Hines Jr. Pearl Johnson Thomas Samuel AZIZA

Members:

Miella Bedell	Michelle Maggiefield
Barbara Benjamin	Alaina Drake Mitchell
Diane Bostic	Gary Mitchell
Barbara Ann Braithwaite	Pam Mitchell
Dorothy Brand	Michelle Monroe
Joann Douglas	L. Qadir
Charlene B. Forde	Loraine Sherod
Pamela Furline	Gerald Small
Rasheda George	Dianne Smith
Nancy L. Grant	Pamela Smith-Watson
Nancy K. Grant	Caroline Taylor
Sugar Harris	Chelsea Taylor
Catherine Hayes	Kathleen Taylor
Keri Hayes	Wendy Thompson
Anabella Hillburn	Jeanette Wilson
Helen Horne	Harold Williams
Rosalind Hyatt	Rhonda Williams
Dana Johnson	Sharon Williams

Howard Hines Jr., President - 2001 - 2004

Second President Howard Hines Jr., a native of Chicago, Illinois attended Jackson State University in Jackson, Mississippi receiving his Bachelor of Arts degree in Speech Communication with a discipline in Communicative Disorders. Howard relocated to New York where he received his Master's degree in Deafness Rehabilitation from New York University and subsequently acquired a second master's of Social Work from Hunter College. He also completed an  Interpreter's Training Program at the New York Society for the Deaf.

He has served as freelance sign language interpreter appearing on Broadway and several off-Broadway shows. He considered himself a "Musical Sign Language Artist" an honor bestowed upon him from the Black Deaf community. Howard has worked with Empowerment Specialist Iyanla Vanzant and has interpreted for such dignitaries as President Clinton and Nelson Mandela.

Howard has been a mentor, supporter and encourager for many aspiring interpreters and those in our African American/Black Deaf, Hearing Interpreting Community and during his tenure as President, he worked as the Director of the Deaf and Hard of Hearing Programs at New York City Technical College in Brooklyn and as an Adjunct Professor for NYC Technical College and the College of New Rochelle teaching American Sign Language.

Howard's four-year tenure as President focused on skill development, certification and community outreach.

YEAR 2001 - 45 Financial members

Officers:

President:	Howard Hines Jr.
Vice President	Christine Dudley
Secretary	Nancy Grant
Asst. Secretary	Diane Bostic
Treasurer	Carol Broughton
Asst. Treasurer	Chevon Spencer
Member-at-Large	JoAnn Douglas
Member-at-Large	Celeste Owens
Member-at-Large	Dianne Smith
Member-at-Large	Linda Wilson

Members:

Rickey Abraham
AZIZA
Miella Bedell
Barbara Benjamin
Barbara-Anne Braithwaite
Karen A. Brown
Joan Canada
Sabrina Caver
Patricia Davis
Samuel Dorch
Vanessa J. Dorch
Marilyn Edwards
Adrienne Ghyll
Nancy Gray

J. Delores Hart
Catherine Hayes
Keri Lynn Hayes
Rhonda Holdip

Helen Horne
Rosalind Hyatt
Dana Johnson
Pearl Johnson
Sharon Johnson
A. J. Jones
Tavoria Kellam
Cathy Markland
Vicki McMillan
Monique Merritt
Michelle Monroe
Caroline Taylor
Kathleen Taylor
Elinora
Ward-DeCambra
Caroll Whitefield
Harold Williams
Rhonda Williams

YEAR 2002 - 51 Financial members

Officers:

President	Howard Hines Jr.
Vice President	Christine Dudley
Secretary	Nancy Grant
Asst. Secretary	Diane Bostic
Treasurer	Carol Broughton
Asst. Treasurer	Chevon Spencer
Member-at-Large	JoAnn Douglas
Member-at-Large	Celeste Owens
Member-at-Large	Dianne Smith
Member-at-Large	Linda Wilson

Members:

Miella Bedell	Robin LaMour
Barbara Benjamin	Iesha McCrea
Linda Bradley	Dion McCray
Dorothy Brand	Vicki McMillan
Joan Canada	Michelle Melbourne
Jacqueline Carter	Alaina Drake Mitchell
Pat Davis	Pamela Mitchell
Jenny Figaro	Rhea Modeste
Charlene B. Forde	Michelle Monroe
Nancy Gray	Nicole A. Morgan
Catherine Hayes	Roberta Reid
Keri Hayes	Janice Rimler
Anabella Hillburn	Lillie Rosario
Cheryl Holder	Nancy Simmons
Rosalind Hyatt	Gerald Small
Dana Johnson	Pam Smith-Watson

Gabrielle Johnson

Sharon Johnson

A. J. Jones

Tavoria Kellam   Paulette
Knarr

Jose Suarez

Kathleen Taylor

Harold Williams

Sharon Williams

YEAR 2003 - 22 Financial members

Officers:

President:	Howard Hines Jr.
Vice President	Christine Dudley
Secretary	A. J. Jones
Asst. Secretary	Miella Bedell
Treasurer	Carol Broughton
Asst. Treasurer	Joan Canada
Member-at-Large	JoAnn Douglas
Member-at-Large	Celeste Owens
Member-at-Large	Dianne Smith
Member-at-Large	Linda Wilson

Members:

Barbara A. Braithwaite	Dion McCray
Catherine Hayes	Michelle Monroe
Keri Hayes	Lillie Rosario
Cheryl Holder	Gerald Small
Robin LaMour	Pamela Smith-Watson
Carol Lue-Martin	Harold Williams

YEAR 2004 - 20 Financial members

Officers:

President:	Howard Hines Jr.
Vice President	Christine Dudley
Secretary	A. J. Jones
Asst. Secretary	Miella Bedell
Treasurer	Carol Broughton
Asst. Treasurer	Joan Canada
Member-at-Large	JoAnn Douglas
Member-at-Large	Celeste Owens
Member-at-Large	Dianne Smith
Member-at-Large	Linda Wilson

Members:

Barbara A. Braithwaite	Gerald Small
Patricia Davis	Pamela Smith Watson
Muriel Gaither	Cheryl Thom
Alicia Jones	Malika Whitney
Michelle Monroe	Harold Williams

Kathleen Taylor, President 2005 - 2007

Third President Kathleen Taylor, a native of Brooklyn, earned her Bachelor of Arts in Biology from Hofstra University and her Master of Arts from New York University in Rehabilitation Counseling Specializing in Deafness. She has earned dual certification from the National Registry of Interpreters for the Deaf (CI/CT) and a certification from  the National Association of the Deaf for sign language interpreting & transliteration (NAD IV).

She has interpreted for Broadway, off-Broadway and regional theatre performances. She has interpreted for highly respected authors, political, social, civic and religious leaders. She was always an advocate for aspiring sign language interpreters, assisting in their growth as professionals for the profession of interpreting.

Kathleen has interpreted in medical, psychiatric, rehabilitation and academic settings. She also has extensive experience as a Mental Health Therapist focusing on under-served and over-looked populations such as the Deaf community, families within the foster care system and survivors of domestic and substance abuse. She prides herself as being resourceful for the needs of the Deaf community.

Kathleen also held several interesting positions while interpreting part-time at night and weekends. She received extensive experience as a Vocational Rehabilitation Counselor for the NYS Education Department and various non-profit organizations in NYC. She was also the Director of an academic program for Deaf Adults from foreign countries who needed to learn ASL, English and American Culture.

During her tenure, as President, Kathleen married Jonathan Taylor and they became parents of a daughter Raven Savannah.

Kathleen's three-year tenure as President focused on increasing chapter membership, professionalism and professional skill development. Prior to her tenure as President, she was elected and served as Eastern Regional Representative of NAOBI, Inc.

YEAR 2005 - 47 members

Officers:

President:	Kathleen D. Taylor
Vice President	A. J. Jones
Secretary	Uneeda Williams
Asst. Secretary	Michelle Monroe
Treasurer	Christine Dudley
Asst. Treasurer	Tammy Lane
PMP Coordinator	Dianne Smith
Member-at-Large	Howard Hines Jr.
Member-at-Large	Robin LaMour

Members:

AZIZA	Gabrielle Johnson
Mary Bacheller	Tavoria Kellman
Calvin Bates	Amy Mecker
Miella Bedell	NYC Metro RID
Justeenia Beltran	Grier Ountra
Barbara Benjamin	Celeste Owens
Kim Berger	Piar Reavis
Diane Boyd	Robin Rinaud
Eugene Bourquin	Janice Rimler
Stephanie Bradford	Celeste Sassine
Linda Bradley	Kathy Sciarabba
Carol Broughton	Loraine Sherod
Eleanor Cyrus	Gerald Small
Patricia Dash	Pamela Smith-Watson
Karin Y. Davis	Chelsea Taylor
Michelle Fields	Laura Taylor
Pamela Furline	Christina Trunzo-Mosleh
Kathy Henderson	Trisch Whitfield
Dana Johnson	Sharon Williams

YEAR 2006 - 58 members

Officers:

President:	Kathleen D. Taylor
Vice President	A. J. Jones
Secretary	Uneeda Williams
Asst. Secretary	Michelle Monroe
Treasurer	Christine Dudley
Asst. Treasurer	Tammy Lane
PMP Coordinator	Dianne Smith
Member-at-Large	Howard Hines Jr.
Member-at-Large	Robin LaMour

Members:

Ruth Aleskovsky	Levanda Miller
Charlene B Forde	Mill Neck Interpreting
Miella Bedell	Rhea Ummi Modeste
Kim A. Berger	Denise Mondesir
Diane Bostic	Bill Moody
Linda Bradley	Nicole Morgan
Denessa Brown	NYC Metro RID
Joan Canada	Celeste Owens
Veronica Cooper	Sheila Rabb
Patricia Dash	Robin Rinaud
Lenola Foy	Jenette Rosario
Pamela Furline	Nicole Russell
Emmanuel Garcia	Lashun Rogers
Adrienne Ghyll	Celeste Sassine
Melanie Girshick	Loraine Sherod
Pamela Green	Gerald Small
Ountra Grier	Pamela Smith-Watson
Patrice Harrington	Sorenson Communication

Loquita Harris
Kathy Henderson

Veronica Hibbler
Dana Johnson
Tavoria Kellum
Robin Kelley
Tracey Lorde

Laura Taylor
Christina Trunzo-Mosleh
Veronica Washington
Malika Whitney
Harold Williams
Genevieve Wreh

YEAR 2007 - 26 members

Officers:
President:	Kathleen D. Taylor
Vice President	Robin LaMour
Secretary	Uneeda Williams
Asst. Secretary	Jenette Rosario
Treasurer	Tammy Lane
Asst. Treasurer	Christine Dudley
PMP Coordinator	A. J. Jones
Member-at-Large	Howard Hines Jr.
Member-at-Large	Diane Boyd
Member-at-Large	Patrice Harrington

Members:
Jeanne Aikens	Cheryl Kelly
Pamela Furline	Latisha Mills
Ountra Grier	Michelle Monroe
Sonja Hamlin	Celeste Owens
Kathy Henderson	Robin Renaud
Kettly Henry-Payne	Janice Rimler
V.Felicia Hibbler	Lashun Rogers
Jeff Jaech	Genevieve Wreh

ABOUT THE AUTHOR

Christine Dudley-Daniels, NAOBI-NYC Member and Author

Christine Dudley-Daniels received her Bachelor of Science degree SUNY Empire Saratoga Springs and her Master of Science Social Work Administration degree from Columbia University, NYC. She also completed an American Sign Language program at the New York Society for the Deaf Sign Language Academy.

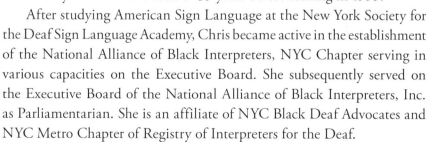

Her professional career began in 1964 working for NYC's Department of Welfare. She held a number of administrative positions serving NYC's Children and Family Services for a total of 35 years before retiring in 1999.

After studying American Sign Language at the New York Society for the Deaf Sign Language Academy, Chris became active in the establishment of the National Alliance of Black Interpreters, NYC Chapter serving in various capacities on the Executive Board. She subsequently served on the Executive Board of the National Alliance of Black Interpreters, Inc. as Parliamentarian. She is an affiliate of NYC Black Deaf Advocates and NYC Metro Chapter of Registry of Interpreters for the Deaf.

Chris views herself more as an advocate than an interpreter. As a Life member of National Action Network NYC Chapter, she established the Interpreter/Advocates Committee and the House of Justice Deaf Club.

An Adjunct Professor with the City University of New York City, Chris teaches American Sign Language as an accredited course. She also serves as Director of Canaan Baptist Church of Christ's Deaf Ministry.

She is a published author having written "Testimony of Faith" (Martin Luther King Fellow's Press, NY 2001), and as a Silver-Life member of Alpha Kappa Alpha Sorority, Tau Omega Chapter in the village of Harlem, she co-authored "The Legacy of the Pacesetters of Tau Omega Chapter: A History of Timeless Service to the Harlem Community and Beyond" (Authorhouse Publisher 2014)

For her volunteer public service, she is the recipient of a number of awards and citations: ***Pearl of Excellence Award*** from North Atlantic Regional Director, Alpha Kappa Alpha Sorority, Inc. ***National Sojourner Truth Meritorious Service Award*** from the National Association of Negro Business and Professional Women's Clubs, Inc. ***Key to Harlem,*** from the Honorable Theresa Freeman, *State Committee Woman/District Leader;* ***President's Choice Award*** from the National Alliance of Black Interpreters, Inc. ***Graduate Good Citizen of the Year Award*** from the North Atlantic Regional Director, Alpha Kappa Alpha Sorority, Inc; ***Women of Excellence Award*** from National Action Network NYC; ***Celebrating Differentabilities Award*** from Deaf Dance Jam Workshop, Inc.; ***Woman of the Year Award*** from Canaan Baptist Church of Christ; ***House of Justice Award*** from National Action Network NYC; ***Unsung Hero Award*** from Canaan Baptist Church; ***Outstanding Volunteer Services*** from Teen Age Services Act, NYC.

She is a wife, mother and grandmother residing with her husband Jack Daniels in the village of Harlem.

ACKNOWLEDGEMENTS

The author would like to thank the following persons for their support and assistance in completing the book.

Celeste Owens, First President	Editing
Howard Hines Jr. Second President	Editing
Kathleen Taylor, Third President	Editing
Melissa Lockley, Current President	Proof Reader
Doris Conner	Proof Reader
A.J. Jones	Proof Reader
Harold Williams, Jr.	Photography
John Cunningham	Photography